Public Participation and Sustainable Development Comparing European Experiences

"PESTO PAPERS 1"

Edited by Andrew Jamison and Per Østby

Public Participation and Sustainable Development
Comparing European Experiences,
PESTO PAPERS 1

ISBN   87-7307-595-0

Copyright   Aalborg Universitetsforlag and
the Authors

Published by Aalborg Universitetsforlag

Printed   Thy Bogtryk og Offset

Distribution Aalborg Universitetsforlag
Badehusvej 16
9000 Aalborg
Phone 9813 0915
Fax no 9813 4915

Foreword

These papers have been written within the research project, Public Participation and Environmental Science and Technology Policy Options (PESTO), which is supported by the Nordic Environmental Research Program (1996-97) and the European Commission's research program on Targeted Socio-Economic Research (TSER) from 1996 to 1998. We are pleased that two of the "partners" in the European project, Lancaster University in the United Kingdom and the University of Twente in the Netherlands, have contributed to this report, even though this review of national experiences is formally not included in the European version of the project.

Our objective in the project is to examine both the new social networks that are being constructed in environmental science and technology in different European countries, and to see how the broader public interest is being taken into account. The specific objectives of the project are:

1) to contrast and compare national experiences in network-building and policy doctrine reform in terms of specific contextual factors, notably institutional traditions, policy styles, and emerging environmental awareness; 2) to analyze and evaluate the effectiveness of the different ways of organizing networks between universities, research institutes and business and government; and 3) to analyze the various ways of involving the public into environmental science and to assess to what extent public participation influences flexibility, competence building and accountability.

These papers represent the results of the first phase of our research. The project itself will continue until the end of 1998. As project coordinator, I would like to express my appreciation to the authors of the papers, as well as to all of those who have commented and offered advice. I also thank Dorthe Andersen at Aalborg University for her assistance.

Aalborg, Denmark in early May 1997

Andrew Jamison

Contents

Introduction

Since the mid-1980s science and technology policy within the environmental field has changed character. On the one hand, environmental s&t policy has been affected by the general changes that have taken place throughout European science and technology policy: the shift towards increased international cooperation and decreased direct state control and the emergence of a new "mode" of knowledge production transcending traditional disciplinary and institutional boundaries (Gibbons et al 1994). On the other hand, environmental s&t policy has come to be directed to the new global problems of climate change and biodiversity and the new "transnational" constellations of actors - both corporate, intergovernmental and non-governmental - which are seeking to ameliorate them (cf. Jamison 1996). Emphasis during the 1990s has been given to the doctrine of sustainability, to preventive measures and so-called cleaner technologies in environmental research and development, both nationally and internationally (cf. Schot 1992; Wynne 1992). In this as in other areas of science and technology policy, however, each European country has assimilated the new doctrines into its own national "system of innovation."

Science and technology policy in the environmental field can be seen to have gone through five main phases since the 1960s (figure one).

Figure One:
Phases of postwar environmentalism s&t policy

Period	Emphasis
1) pre-68: awakening	public education and debate
2) 69-74: sectorization	institution building/environment as R&D sector
3) 75-80: public mobilization	energy policy
4) 81-86: professionalization	environmental assessment
5) 87-: internationalization	integration/sustainable development

---

In the 1960s, a new range of environmental problems were identified - industrial pollution, atomic radiation, urban sprawl - that tended to supplant traditional conservation issues from most national political agendas. These problems gave rise to a widespread public debate throughout the industrialized countries and, eventually, to a number of policy responses.

The second phase was inspired by the general questioning of industrial society that came in the wake of the student revolts. It was also a period of active institution building. It was then that most industrialized countries established sectorial agencies to deal with environmental protection, and environmental research, education, and even technological development were organized in new institutional forms. Many countries passed stronger environmental legislation, and set up new kinds of courts to decide over cases of environmental pollution. In this phase, the concepts of ecology were transformed into political programs, and at the UN Conference on the Human Environment in Stockholm in 1972, the environment was recognized as a new international policy concern.

We can refer to a third phase of environmental s&t policy from the first oil crisis until about 1980. This was a time when environmentalism had a major impact on national political agendas, especially in relation to energy policy, and when several of the larger national environmental organizations turned into mini-bureaucracies. An important result of the energy debates of the 1970s was a professionalization of environmental concern and an incorporation by the established political structures of what had originally been a somewhat delimited, even marginal political issue. As a result, there was a specialization of knowledge production.

The effect was that, when nuclear energy was removed from many national political agendas in the early 1980s, there was a range of expertise that had previously not existed. In many European countries, there were university departments and research institutes, as well as substantial state bureaucracies that had an institutional interest in environmental problems. From the mid-1980s, as the network-building activities of the new environmental professionals began to be felt, we can legitimately speak of a fifth, or international, phase of environmental science and technology policy, in which global problems have taken over from local problems as the main areas of concern; and the solution to these problems has been characterized, since the report of the World Commission on Environment and Development in 1987, as "sustainable development."

At the same time, many business firms have begun to adopt new methods of clean, or cleaner production, including environmental auditing, recycling of waste products, and more efficient uses of resources and energy in production processes. For some, the shift is seen as a change in production paradigm; increasingly, environmental concern is being integrated into corporate planning and innovation strategies, while management schools are beginning to provide training in environmental economics as well as in the new methods of production.

In many respects, this shift in agenda can be seen as a convergence of interests between environmental organizations, governmental agencies and transnational firms. The promulgation of national and international programs to encourage "cleaner production" in industrial firms has led to the creation of new institutions at universities and engineering schools, and, in many European countries, new departments of environmental management, economics and engineering are being established to provide the professional experts who are to direct the greening of industry (cf. Fischer and Schot, eds 1993).

These shifts have manifested themselves both on a discursive level, where new principles of environmental science and technology are being formulated, as well as on a practical level, where informal networks are serving to link universities, business and government agencies in new configurations. In between, at an intermediary institutional level, policy-makers face fundamental problems in designing appropriate programs and policy measures to move environmental science and technology in more sustainable directions. What is often lacking is sufficient understanding of the relevant factors that shape and/or constrain effective policy response. By comparing national experiences in a systematic way, as well as investigating the social and organizational dynamics of the ongoing transformation processes, our project aims to fill some of those gaps in understanding.

Our research strategy is to move from the general doctrinal level to a more detailed investigation of the emerging networks of innovation in the environmental field. The general structural model of a national policy system, or realm, is drawn from the literature on science and technology policy (cf. Nelson 1993); but while most analysts have focused on the economic aspects of R&D policy, our interest is directed to what might be termed the cultural dimensions of s&t policy. In the model that has been developed, science and technology policy is conceptualized as an arena of interaction between four policy domains, or constituencies - economic, bureaucratic, academic, and civic. These domains are characterized by different ideals of science and technology policy, that is, by different attitudes to the general social functions of science and technology. Each domain also tends to favor particular kinds of policy measures, as well as different types of programs and projects (cf. Elzinga and Jamison 1995). the general perspective can be depicted as in figure two:

Figure Two:
Cultural Tensions in Science and Technology Policy

Policy domain

Dimension	Bureaucratic	Economic	Academic	Civic
Principle	order	growth	enlightenment	democracy
Steering mechanism	planning	commercial	peer review	public assessment
Ethos	formalistic	entrepreneurial	scientific	participatory

In the PESTO project, this model is applied to science and technology policy in the environmental field. We examine the interactions among the different constituencies in particular national settings. Our range of countries includes Britain, where the academic domain has traditionally been dominant in science policy and technology policy has largely been left to the private sector, or economic domain; Sweden and Norway, where the bureaucratic and economic interests are historically strong;

Denmark and the Netherlands, with strong civic traditions, but with different combinations of bureaucratic, economic and academic influences; Italy, with a greater balance among the four policy domains; and Lithuania, struggling to emerge from the bureaucratic order and reinvent academic, economic and civic traditions. By comparing experiences in such a wide range of countries, we hope that it will be possible to distinguish those factors that are nationally, or culturally specific from general historically convergent factors that are at work throughout Europe.

In any case, this first report is an attempt to describe some of the most important features of the national experiences of seven of our eight PESTO countries.

References

Elzinga, Aant and Andrew Jamison (1995) Changing Policy Agendas in Science and Technology, in S Jasanoff, et al, eds, *Handbook of Science and Technology Studies*. Sage

Fischer, Kurt and Johan Schot, eds (1993) *Environmental Strategies for Industry*. Island Press

Gibbons, Michael, et al (1994) *The New Production of Knowledge*. Sage

Jamison, Andrew (1996) The Shaping of the Global Environmental Agenda, in S Lash, et al, eds, *Risk, Environment, Modernity*. Sage

Nelson, Richard (1993) *National Innovation Systems: A Comparative Analysis*. Oxford

Schot, Johan (1992) Constructive Technology Assessment and Technology Dynamics: The Case of Clean Technologies, in *Science, Technology and Human Values* 17 (1).

Wynne, Brian (1992) Uncertainty and Environmental Learning: Reconceiving Science and Policy in the Preventive Paradigm, in *Global Environmental Change*, 2

Sweden: The Dilemmas of Polarization

by Andrew Jamison[*]

1. Introduction

Sweden was one of the first countries in the world to develop a science and technology policy in the area of environmental protection. Several years before the environmental crisis had become a matter of concern in other industrialized countries, Swedish policy makers were considering suitable responses. The Swedish government took initiatives in large-scale systems ecological research, in supporting the development of pollution-control technology, and in reforming environmental administration and legislation already in the 1960s, before most other European countries had even become aware of the new kinds of environmental problems (Jamison et al 1990).

Compared to neighboring countries like Denmark and Norway, Sweden was a pioneer in creating a new kind of research policy sector in the environmental field. Indeed, environmental research and development (R&D) served as an archetypical example of the sectorialization of Swedish research policy during the 1970s, by which the "model" welfare

[*] I would like to thank the members of the Swedish PESTO group, Arni Sverrisson, Magnus Ring and Kees Dekker, for their comments. The paper has drawn on a longer paper that Kees Dekker has produced while a research fellow in Lund.

state extended its range and influence and its tradition of social engineering into previously largely unexplored realms of policy-making (Elzinga 1993). A long historical legacy of nature appreciation and conservation, and a sizeable constituency of environmental researchers among natural scientists, certainly played a role, but the main reason for Sweden's head start over other countries is probably the specific national style of policy making, with a strong and actively interventionist state.

Interestingly enough, the Swedish head start would, at a later stage, come to serve as a constraint to new initiatives in environmental science and technology policy. In the 1990s, Sweden has lagged behind other European countries in supporting programs in pollution prevention and cleaner technology - so-called ecological modernization (Hajer 1995). In many ways, the new approaches have not fit easily into the highly concentrated industrial structure; and they have also come at a time of serious questioning of the Swedish style of policy making, including a retrenchment of the role of the state.

Recently, however, at least some political leaders have proclaimed their intention to improve Sweden's flagging economic situation, and, in particular, reduce the uncharacteristically high levels of unemployment, by creating thousands of new "green jobs", as they are euphemistically referred to in Sweden. Göran Persson, the new prime minister, declared when taking office in early 1996 that Sweden would soon lead the world in the establishment of an "ecologically sustainable society," and in the following year, a series of proposals have been made with the ambition to transform entire sectors of the economy into more sustainable directions, taking what Persson has termed a "great leap forward" for Swedish society.

The government has also decided to begin the controversial process of dismantling the nuclear energy industry, which has been continually delayed since a referendum in 1980 led to a parliamentary decision to phase out the subtantial nuclear energy industry. Persson's proposed use of ecological employment to deal with the deterioration of the Swedish economy has met with heated resistance from conservative politicians and business leaders. The social democratic leader is seen as falling under the influence of an "ecological fundamentalism" emanating from the anti-nuclear Center Party, with which the new government has formed a working alliance. In many respects, the rhetorical tone of the environmental discourse is reminiscent of the energy debate of the 1970s, when the Swedish society was deeply polarized around the nuclear issue. Since then, however, the role of the state has been significantly weakened, and it is highly uncertain that the new state plans will have the impact on the economy that is envisioned by the social democrats.

In regard to public participation, it can be argued that the relative effectiveness with which the Swedish approach "technically fixed" the environmental problems that it was originally set up to deal with has served to keep critical voices outside of the policy-making process; the comparative success of Swedish research and development efforts has apparently made it difficult for non-experts to find a role to play. Swedish environmental science and technology policy has, for the most part, been made by a relatively small number of scientific/technical experts, in alliance with the state authorities and the industrial establishment. There has been little room for the general public or the "environmental movement" to be directly involved.

Environmental expertise has generally been defined in highly instrumental and practical terms, with comparatively little interest in the "softer" components of environmental knowledge that have been much more developed in other countries: environmental social science, technology assessment, environmental ethics. And even though the government has recently formulated a number of far-reaching plans for sustainable development and adopted what might be termed an ecological rhetoric, actual support for practical measures, and for research, development, and competence building, in the new approaches of pollution prevention and cleaner production, is still rather small in Sweden, when compared to countries like Denmark and the Netherlands. Indeed, in the fall of 1996, when the government presented its research policy plan, environmental R&D was one of the many areas that was allocated decreased state funding (Forskning och samhälle 1996). In the Swedish socio-economic order, ecological modernization has primarily been seen as the responsibility of the private sector, while the government's role has been more rhetorical than practical (Lidskog 1996). And, if business leaders continue to oppose the government's ecological rhetoric, the effective implementation of an ecological reconstruction of society seems unlikely.

If the system has been less participatory than elsewhere, throughout the brief history of Swedish environmental science and technology policy, the public has nonetheless been present - in exerting pressure, in protesting, and in proposing policy options. Because the public debate about nuclear energy was so intense and divisive in the 1970s, however, the environmental discourse in Sweden has taken on a polarized coloration, a more antagonistic shade of green. In any case, at the present time, the environmental movement seems to be largely excluded from the realm of science and technology policy making, both in the private sector, as well as in the new state plans. It is thus interesting to trace the development of environmental science and technology policy in Sweden, and see how and why public participation has changed over the years, from exclusion in the 1960s to various forms of inclusion in the 1970s and 1980s and back again, in the 1990s, to a new period of exclusion.

2. The Swedish National Policy Style

In Sweden, the state has historically played an active role in social and economic life, and scientists and other experts have long served as "policy intellectuals" to a somewhat greater extent than in other countries (Eyerman et al 1987). Particularly in the early 20th century, when the Swedish government initiated a number of welfare-oriented economic policies, the involvement of university professors and other academics in the policy-making process was significant. Through Gunnar and Alva Myrdal and other intellectuals, Swedish social-democracy in the 1930s was strongly influenced by the ideas of American progressive reformers, but there was also an indigenous tradition of pragmatism and state service among intellectuals that was mobilized in the making of the so-called Swedish model. Also important was the strength of corporativism in Sweden, the effective channels of communication and negotiation that were established between the state and the private sector, and between employers and employees. The highly organized character of Swedish social life is also noteworthy in this regard (both employers and employees, for instance, have central federations that, until recently, conducted negotiations for most of the industrial economy). Many of these features have been fundamentally transformed over the past 20 years, however, both because of an increasing political polarization but also because of Sweden's joining the European Union.

In many ways, the distinctive Swedish national policy style dates back to the state building efforts of the 16th century. The absolutist period in Sweden was unusual, when compared to the other smaller countries of Europe, in that Sweden's kings grounded their military expenditures and their great power ambitions on an ideology of gothic grandeur articulated, among others, by Olof Rudbeck, a professor at the university of Uppsala. Rudbeck was also an early policy adviser for both the economic and administrative arms of the emerging state apparatus (Jamison 1982). A kind of alliance between what might be termed academic and bureaucratic policy domains thus was established at a very early stage in Sweden's modern history. At the same time, economic and civic policy domains have come under the influence of the state to a somewhat greater extent than elsewhere. Through the centuries, these various domains, or "policy cultures", have developed different ideas or principles of policy-making as well as different norm and value systems in relation to scientific and technical research.

In Sweden, the historical experience has left a legacy of "statism" and corporativism that has colored, in significant ways, the making of environmental science and technology policy. Already in the 17th century, there emerged a number of "offices" or agencies to administer various aspects of national life - from mining to forestry, from defense to education. A relatively strong state bureaucracy came to exercise control over areas of social life which in many other countries were long left in private hands. In particular, the natural environment, and the variety of natural resources with which Sweden, compared to many other European countries, was so richly endowed, became an early state responsibility. And the "rational" use or exploitation of these resources became an important topic of investigation for scientists and other experts at a comparatively early period.

The colorful reports of Carl von Linné, or Linneaus, as he is known abroad, in the mid-18th century, detailing the resources to be found in the various regions of Sweden, as well as the productive practices in which those resources were put to use, continue to be read today for both enlightenment and pleasure. Along with his more explicitly scientific writings, Linneaus' travelogues are among the first examples of environmental science in Sweden, and have served as models for ecological research in other countries, as well. Indeed, the historian Donald Worster has characterized Linneaus as one of the main precursors of the science of ecology, contrasting his "imperialist" approach to ecology to the "arcadian" approach of the English pastor Gilbert White (Worster 1977). Ecology in Sweden was already in the 18th century linked, by Linneaus and others, to the needs of the emerging bourgeois, or industrial order.

Linneaus was one of the founding members, in 1739, of the Swedish Academy of Sciences, which, perhaps more than any other institution in the country, has served as an organizational conduit for scientists to take part in state policy making. The Academy of Sciences, and later the Academy of Engineering Science (IVA), which was founded during the first world war, have provided expert advice in a wide range of policy areas. They have served to represent the academic community in what has become an increasingly formalized and comparatively well organized system of policy deliberation. In the postwar period, the role of the academies has been somewhat weakened, as new organizations and institutions have emerged within the academic community, but their influence remains strong, and serves to accentuate the hierarchical and elitist nature of Swedish (scientific/technological) policy making. In any case, at an early stage, an alliance, and a number of functional working relations, were established between the state bureaucracy and the academic community.

This academic-bureaucratic alliance has been extremely influential in the making of environmental science and technology policy. In the 1940s and 1950s, when the social democratic government was developing the so-called Swedish model of state intervention and active labor market policy, environmental issues were given significant public attention. In what was to become a characteristic of the Swedish approach to these matters, policy making centered around the apparatus of "royal investigative commissions" consisting of representatives of the relevant policy constituencies meeting together to deliberate on the appropriate measures to be taken. It was such a commission in the 1950s that led to the reorganization of environmental administration. And it was an investigative commission on environmental research that led to the emergence of a particular science and technology policy sector in the environmental field in the 1970s.

Investigative commissions provide a means for different actors to negotiate and reach consensus over legislative proposals and administrative reforms. But their mode of operation is top-down and hierarchical, rather than participatory and democratic. The way the system works is that the commission reports are circulated to a number of interest organizations for comment before becoming transformed into legislative proposals. Participation is thus at best reactive, and there is no requirement for the parliament or government to take the solicited comments into account. Originally created to provide "expert" advice to the king, the commissions now serve to filter expert knowledge into the state policy making apparatus. In most areas of public life, these commissions play a central role in preparing new kinds of policy measures, and the round of commenting is meant to provide a public, or democratic, legitimacy for reform proposals. But as has been noted recently, the deliberative Swedish system, at least in the area of environmental protection, has tended to exclude groups or "actors" that represent an interest that is considered outside of the official policy-making community. In the words of the political scientist Lennart Lundqvist, perhaps Sweden's leading analyst of environmental policy, there is an "iron triangle" of experts, bureaucrats and industrial leaders that dominates environmental policy making, and within which there has developed a "consensus concerning what is to be considered environmentally relevant competence." After investigating the distribution of participants in a variety of commissions, delegations, and committees in the area of environmental policy during the 1990s, Lundqvist concludes that the consensus that has been reached within this triangle "excludes alternative points of view and alternative competences, ie, those that are to be found in environmental organizations" (Lundqvist 1996).

The general public has historically been poorly represented in this Swedish political and administrative system. In the 19th century, as elsewhere in Europe, there emerged popular movements among the farmers and the industrial working class, but in Sweden these movements rather quickly became institutionalized in the form of political parties, the Center party representing the farmers and the social democratic party representing the industrial workers. It has been primarily through the formalized parliamentary system that Swedish democracy has offered opportunities for public participation in policy-making. On the other hand, the Swedish legal framework has ensured public access to nature, and, for that matter, to the state bureaucracy, as a way to guarantee public acceptance and support, in general as a means to legitimize the strong state role in economic affairs. The ombudsman, serving to mediate between the state and the public, is a uniquely Swedish institution, as is the tradition of *allemansrätt*, the officially sanctioned free access to nature that dates back to the early modern era. The notion of the "people's home" that was adopted as a kind of slogan by the social democratic prime minister, Per Albin Hansson, in the 1930s, similarly rests on a long pattern of self-conscious paternalism in the state's dealings with the citizenry. The state bureaucracy in Sweden has sought to serve as the public's protector, first against the landed aristocracy, and, in the 20th century, against the modern version of the aristocracy, the large corporate industrial firms. In recent years, however, due to a professionalization of politics and an increasing "Europeanization" of policy-making, the Swedish political culture seems to be losing something of its distinctiveness, and at least some bureaucrats and policy-makers seem more interested in joining their European colleagues in a new cosmopolitan aristocracy than in protecting the public from corporate power.

It has also been the case that the extremely international, or "globalized" Swedish economy has been increasingly forced to follow patterns and rules set outside the national boundaries. As elsewhere, international market competitiveness rather than national distinctiveness - including a traditional interest in environmental protection - has become the main dirving force behind science and technology policy. And with declining economic fortunes, the role of the state has been diminished by successive governments from both sides of the political spectrum. The result has been that environmental improvements have not been given as much attention as in other countries, where firms, often in alliance with public authorities, have seen somewhat greater economic opportunities in the calls for sustainable development.

3. Phase One: Constitution, 1960s- early 1970s

Swedish environmental science and technology policy can be seen to have gone through three main periods since its formation in the late 1960s as a separate policy sector (figure one). The first period can be termed constitution, and marked the coming of a special sectorial approach to environmental research and development. As opposed to those in the fledgling environmental movement who argued for a new socio-economic "paradigm", a more ecological approach to economics and social development, Swedish policy makers put into place an interconnected system of institutions, organizations and interpersonal networks.

The Environmental Protection Board, created in 1967 as the world's first environmental agency, brought into one centralized authority a range of responsibilities that had previously been spread in many agencies (Lundqvist 1971). The EPB, and the various local authorities, sought to develop pragmatic solutions to the pollution and waste problems that were grabbing so much public attention and concern. Subsidies were given to pollution control equipment, sewage treatment plants, and techniques for monitoring and even environmental restoration. One of the largest environmental research projects involved the restoration of polluted lakes, by testing new techniques of cleaning and purefication.

Environmental courses were created at the universities in order to train the new cadres of regulators and researchers. Science became an instrument of control in the name of environmental protection. A new policy sector was created without challenging the fundamental paradigmatic assumptions of the dominant political culture. Indeed, in the pursuit of pollution control and "keeping Sweden clean" - as the phraseology went at the time - a range of new opportunities were established for scientists, engineers, business managers and public authorities

There were pioneering activities in the 1960s in all the relevant policy domains, or constituencies, with the state playing a strong coordinating role. As in many other areas of public policy, royal commissions were highly influential in reforming environmental policy making in general and environmental science and technology policy in particular. The Natural

Resources Commission, with representatives from government, industry, and universities, rewrote the environmental research policy agenda with its report of 1967. No longer would the various components of environmental R&D be dealt with in isolation; there needed to be a systematization of environmental R&D, and much stronger attention given to the new approaches of ecosystem ecology. Even though there was not to be a unified environmental research agency, the various components would be linked together in a conscious plan of attack, and a systematic conception of nature - and of ecological research - would be given pride of place (Jamison 1973). This is what the historian of science Thomas Söderqvist later referred to as a program for the "ecologization of modern Sweden." From previously being "merry naturalists", ecologists, as Söderqvist puts it, had become the "saviours" of the nation (Söderqvist 1986).

In a sense, the system that began to take form in the 1960s offered something to everyone without satisfying anyone completely: it represented a consensual compromise. The economic policy domain was given its own research institute, the Institute for Water and Air Pollution Research, and the newly established Board for Technical Development, within the Department of Industry, was charged with supporting environmental control technology as one of its responsibilities. Applied, regulatory-oriented research was placed within the Environmental Protection Board, and the university scientists who had done so much to bring the new range of issues to public attention, were given increased funding, primarily for ecological research. The Natural Science Research Council created an ecology committee, and large-scale projects in systems ecology - with participants from a number of scientific fields and different universities - were funded by the new committee. Systems ecology brought to Sweden the cybernetic approach to biology that Howard Odum had developed in the United States, and, for several years, it came to dominate ecological research in Swedish universities. The labor movement was also given a role to play in the emerging environmental R&D sector with the development of funds and later councils and institutions for research in occupational health and safety: the so-called working environment.

For a few brief years, Sweden came to stand as a kind of international pilot plant, a place for developing innovations in environmental science, technology, and administration. The political response to the environmental challenges of pollution, urban expansion, and traffic congestion had been quick and apparently effective. And the new issues had become integrated into the Swedish administrative and organizational apparatus, while not affecting the twin assumptions of economic growth and corporativist consensus building. Environmental science and technology were simply added onto the R&D system as a new area of specialization, and a new economic-industrial branch of pollution control equipment and sewage treatment plants established itself. Sweden's environmental problems would be controlled and managed through what has been termed an "end-of-pipe" approach.

4. Phase Two: Institution-building, 1970s- mid 1980s

The debate over nuclear energy had a fundamental impact on this newly constituted environmental science and technology policy sector. It accentuated tensions among the various policy domains, and, not least, between political parties. It led to new kinds of policy and administrative initiatives. Most importantly for our purposes, it brought about major transformations in the relations between policy makers and the general public, caused by the emergence of a new social movement primarily around the issue of nuclear energy.

As in other European countries, a new environmental movement had emerged in Sweden in the 1960s, but, until the nuclear energy debate, it had remained marginal to national politics and science and technology policy making (Jamison et al 1990). On the one hand, there was the strong presence of an older environmental "movement", represented by the national conservation society (*Sveriges Naturskyddsföreningen*, SNF) and its youth group, the field biologists, which had effectively been integrated into the policy system already in the 1930s, when society experts were invited to take part in a royal investigative commission. By the 1960s, the field biologists had become a more radical and outspoken part of an emergent youth movement, and these young conservationists conducted a number of demonstrations against environmental pollution, particulartly in the seas and forests. When Rachel Carson's book *Silent Spring* was published in Swedish in 1963, the conservation society officially took on the new pollution issues as part of its concern, and, in its formal, legalistic way, put pressure on the state authorities to strengthen the environmental control effort, while the field biologists increasingly meshed into the new, more activist environmental movement that developed in the wake of the student protests against the war in Vietnam.

This wing of the emergent movement was more decentralized, and based on a wide variety of local protests against particular development projects: parking lots, airports, industrial pollution, food additives, etc. Björn Gillberg, a biologist in Uppsala, became a public spokesman for this locally-based movement by writing articles in the newspapers and appearing on television, criticizing the impotence of the new environmental control bureaucracy and challenging the "end-of-pipe" approach to environmental control. He and many others in the new environmental action groups opposed not merely the consequences of technology, but also many of the technological products and projects themselves. In the early 1970s, there were major protest actions in

Stockholm against a new subway station, in Gothenburg against a new parking facility, and in southern Sweden against Malmö's new airport in the countryside. By the mid 1970s activists had banded together into two competing national organizations: one, the National Federation of Environmental Groups (*Miljövårdgruppernas riksförbund*, MIGRI), led by Gillberg and another, the Environmental Union (*Miljöförbundet*, MF), that explicitly sought to link environmental issues to questions of international solidarity. In 1972, a Swedish affiliate to the international organization, Friends of the Earth, was created in Stockholm, and was actively involved in alternative meetings at that summer's United Nations Conference on the Human Environment, but it never became a significant national force, as it did in other European countries. In 1995, MF and Friends of the Earth merged into one organization, that now stands almost alone as an organized radical force in Swedish environmental politics.

A significant factor in Sweden was the "greening" of the oppositional Center Party in the early 1970s, and especially the emergence of the Center Party leader, Thorbjörn Fälldin, as one of the most vocal opponents of nuclear energy. There was thus, at a comparatively early stage, a parliamentary dispute over energy policy, which gave the anti-nuclear movement a legitimacy that it didn't have in other countries until much later in the decade. But the Center party opposition to nuclear energy also meant that there was somewhat less room for extra-parliamentary groups to play in Sweden than was the case in other countries. In any case, the convergence of parliamentary and extra-parliamentary opponents to nuclear energy helped propel energy policy onto the national political agenda. From the time of the oil crisis of 1974 until the referendum on nuclear energy in 1980, there was an ongoing national energy debate that was to have major implications for environmental science and technology policy.

The energy debate led to a number of new investigative commissions, and with them the creation of a range of new experts in the various aspects of energy technology and energy policy. New programs in renewable energy research and technological experimentation with new forms of energy distiribution and conservation, as well as expanded R&D efforts in nuclear safety and energy planning all served to create opportunities for new kinds of professional expertise. As part of the most substantial investigative commission, the Energy Commission, the extra-parliamentary environmental movement was given funding to produce its own alternative energy plan, and there was thus even a certain opportunity for a "counter-expertise" to emerge in energy politics. In preparing the alternative plan, however, the environmental movement was forced to behave in much the same way as its established opponents; a steering group, with representatives from the field biologists, MF, and Friends of the Earth, was created with the then chairman of MF (now a social democratic environmental politician) charged with the official, day-to-day coordinating work, based in an office at the Department of Industry. MALTE, as the alternative plan was called, became a source of professionalization within the environmental movement; and many of the "counter-experts" who contributed to the plan would later become professional energy experts and/or policy makers. In this respect, the environmental movement provided, as it still does, a kind of schooling in environmental politics, which, at least for some, has been able to lead to professional careers in environmental sciemce, engineering, management, or policy.

This politically-motivated activity also had repercussions in the universities, where at least some academics joined with activists in organizing conferences and meetings. Unlike the situation in other countries, however, this academic activism proved difficult to institutionalize; it was only in Gothenburg that university authorities permitted the establishing of an "alternative" institution in the 1970s - the Center for Interdisciplinary Studies - which, in the 1980s, divided into a Department of Human Ecology and a unit for human technology, where a number of critical projects and courses have been conducted. Interest in alternative energy technology, and alternative uses of energy, did develop at the technical universities and at some of the people's high schools, but, unlike the situation in neighboring Denmark, these interests proved difficult to organize effectively. There was a major exhibition on alternative technology at the Modern Museum in Stockholm in 1976, but it proved to be a one-shot affair. Aside from isolated research projects at some of the architecture departments at the technical universities, there was little organized research in Sweden devoted to alternative technology, either within the academic or civic policy domains..

For the most part, the expertise that was generated emerged within, or was quickly incorporated into, the bureaucratic and economic policy domains. Within the state bureaucracy, a number of new agencies and committees were established - a Board for Energy Production, a committee for Energy Systems Analysis within the newly established Council for Research Coordination, and various organs for energy research within other sectorial bodies. In general terms, Swedish science and technology policy increased significantly in the course of the 1970s; well over 50 new funding agencies and committees were created within the different government ministries (Elzinga 1993). In many ways, energy R&D was the spearhead of a multifaceted process of expansionism. But there were also other environmental research areas, like transportation and working environment (occupational health and safety), which benefited from the sectorializing ambitions. Even the future was given an agency. In 1972, there was created, at the government level, a "secretariat for future studies" following an investigative commission headed by Alva Myrdal, and the new agency, among other things, sponsored a major future study on energy and society, which brought both engineers, physicists and social scientists into the field of energy research. The research programs in energy conservation and renewable energy led to the establishment of new academic institutions at universities and technical colleges, and, as in other countries, to a range of new businesses and consulting firms. There was thus not merely a bureaucratic expansion, but an academic and economic expansion, as well.

Compared to many other European countries, Sweden concentrated a good deal more of its R&D funding and its collective public attention on energy issues, and in particular, to the pros and cons of nuclear energy. This led to a kind of "overkill": after the referendum, it was difficult to mobilize activists around new environmental issues, and the concentration of attention also served to give an impression that the experts had the situation under control. The result, in any case, was that, in the 1980s, there was a range of new experts in energy related science and technology.

But why was there such a focus on nuclear energy? For one thing, nuclear energy had been a major component of social democratic industrial and economic policy, and major firms were involved, as were many leaders of the academic and industrial establishments. It was thus a matter of some prestige, and it proved difficult for the ruling social democratic party to renounce its nuclear energy program; instead, they were willing to invest substantial resources in trying to make it safer and convince the population that it was the most appropriate energy form.

Opposition to nuclear energy also proved to have symbolic value, however, in bringing into question many assumptions of the entire postwar Swedish model; and it managed to mobilize the non-socialist opposition in the election of 1975, so that a non-social democratic government could come to power for the first time in over 30 years. The nuclear issue led to a deep polarization in Swedish public life, and inspired a kind of backlash in the form of conservative ideologists and corporate leaders who questioned the rationality and the motivations of anti-nuclear activists. The virulence of the debate also led to no real change in energy policy, or in the broader orientation of industry, as was the case in other countries. In power, the Center Party managed to achieve very little, since it was forced to rule in alliance with the conservative parties that did not oppose nuclear energy. The result was a referendum that was held in 1980, but which, by offering three choices to the voters, left the verdict unclear. While the referendum managed to take the issue off the political agenda, it left the actual resolution of the nuclear issue to experts.

5. Phase Three - Reconstitution, mid 1980s- 1990s

By the early 1980s, Sweden thus had a sizeable environmental research and development sector, which had been vastly expanded to include a number of new energy agencies and institutions. Expertise in environmental management and energy policy was also widely distributed through the state bureacracy and the large corporations. And there was also a number of new consulting firms in environmental engineering and energy technology that had, as it were, vested interest in environmental R&D. At the same time, a new kind of professional and international environmental movement had come to Sweden in the guise of Greenpeace. The aftermath of the referendum led to a decline in the extra-parliamentary environmental movement, and the disappointment with the Center Party led to the formation of a new parliamentary Environmental, later called Green Party. The reconstitution that took place in Sweden, as well as in most other European countries, from the second half of the

1980s, thus involved a somewhat different constellation of actors than had been involved in the period of constitution.

One important new "actor" has emerged from within the private sector. Although Swedish industry was comparatively late to take up the new ideas about pollution prevention and cleaner technology, that have been widely propagated in most other European countries, much of the new R&D effort in recent years has been devoted to environmental improvements in industry. In 1993, a new Foundation for Strategic Environmental Research was created to support large-scale projects involving collaboration between universities and industry in the area of "sustainable development". At the same time, several other foundations were established, with money taken by the then conservative government from the controversial wage-earner funds, which the social democrats had created in the 1980s. These foundations are charged with funding strategic industrial research and technological competence building and are run as private foundations, with decisions taken primarily by representatives of industrial firms and the engineering, or technological sciences. One small foundation supports the newly-established International Institute for Industrial Environmental Economics at the Technical University in Lund. And at the other technical universities and business schools, a range of projects and courses are being instituted in environmental management and economics, many with the support of the new foundations.

Compared to many other European countries, however, these new initiatives have come relatively late, and have had trouble being integrated into established disciplines and institutions. The example of the institute in Lund, which lies outside of the traditional disciplinary structure and has its own outside funding, is all too typical of the Swedish reconstitution process. The lion's share of environmental research and development work continues to be channeled through the Environmental Protection Board and the other sectorial agencies - in energy, transportation, waste treatment, occupational health, regional planning, construction, etc. - which were created in the 1970s. There is a need for greater coordination among the myriad of agencies and committees, particularly between the older state bodies and the newer private foundations; and there is also a need for greater integration of the various efforts, both old and new, into the "non-environmental" sectors. As things stand now, the environmental science and technology system remains a sector that, while growing, still has relatively little impact on the main priorities of Swedish science and technology policy, which, as in most other countries, are focused around the so-called advanced technologies: information technology, biotechnology, industrial materials.

Recently, the Swedish government has launched a number of initiatives to give a concrete form to the "ecological adaptation" that Göran Persson called for when he became the new prime minister. There has been created a state delegation, or committee, for an "ecologically sustainable development" and another for the "stimulation of environmentally adapted technology". The delegation for sustainable development, led by the Minister of Environment Anna Lindh, has as its task to "formulate a platform for the government policy for an ecologically sustainable society and to create a broad and long-term investment programme". The government has expressed the intention, as expressed by Persson in his government policy statement, to modernise housing, construction, the energy system, the production system, the transportation system, the water and sewage system in order to become "ecologically sustainable". Conservative politicians and economists have compared the plans to the social engineering that was so prominent in the 1940s and 1950s, when suburbs and the modern infrastructure were established in Sweden, through strong centralised planning that has since gone out of fashion. That kind of planning, it is argued, can no longer function in a society that is so strongly integrated into the international market. (cf Berggren 1997).

The delegation for environmental technology has as its task to develop a strategy to introduce new technology and processes which can "contribute to solving specific problems with large social relevance as well as create development and renewal opportunities for the industry" (Delegation for Support of Environmentally-adapted Technology 1996). In addition to solving environmental problems and reducing the use of natural resources, the environmental technologies are considered to contribute to the attempt of the government to create new jobs. The delegation has not defined very precisely what it means by environmental technology, however; that is left to the companies and technological research institutes. In Sweden, however, there has been little attempt to support "cleaner technologies" or techniques of pollution prevention as in many other European countries. In its working document, the delegation prioritises the transport sector, the building sector, the agricultural sector as well as soil sanitation. In cooperation with involved actors, the delegation's main activity will be the purchase of environmental technology.

Technology procurement is also the main mechanism used by the office for more effective energy use at the Swedish Board for Technical and Industrial Development (*NUTEK*). The delegation for environmental technology is related to this office. The chairperson of the delegation for the stimulation of environmentally adapted technology, Birgitta Böhlin, is employed at the Materials Agency of Swedish Defence FMV which is one of the largest state purchasers of technology, and has played a leading role in Swedish technology policy (cf. Jamison 1991). A possible demand group will be created to formulate what need exists for environmental adapted technology, after which tenders will be invited. In addition to bringing together companies and universities/research institutions, the delegation will attempt to stimulate the demand for environmental technology through for instance information activities and pilot projects. The government has also invested about 2.5 billion SEK in programmes with an environmental profile which are supposed to create "green jobs". During a period of five years, projects will be supported which "improve the environment, stimulate the use of environmental technology and increase employment".

In early 1997, the social democratic government announced that it had reached an agreement with the Center Party on nuclear energy. The agreement entails that the first nuclear reactor at Barsebäck will be dismantled by July 1998, with other reactors following thereafter (Ministry of Economic Affairs 1997). In the agreement, however, no final date is mentioned for the dismantling of all reactors, because of possible problems for "employment, wealth, competitiveness and the environment". The agreement emphasizes the need for a plan to adapt the energy system:

> The goal is to achieve an ecologically and
> economically sustainable energy provision mainly
> based upon renewable energy sources.....

According to the energy agreement, the Swedish electricity system should become largely self sufficient, based primarily on domestically produced electricity. A new agency was to be established with the responsibility for the adaptation of the energy system. In a newspaper article, Göran Persson and Olof Johansson, leader of the Center Party, argued that the introduction of the ecological sustainable society for them is no "utopia", in which modern technology would have no role to play. The ecological adaptation is rather presented as something that will stimulate new jobs and new technology.

In spite of this, the energy and environmental plans of the government have caused an intensive public debate in Sweden, with one of the early attacks being a highly publicized open letter signed by over 100 business leaders. The leaders of industry accuse the government of seriously weakening the operating conditions for a competitive industry. According to the chairperson of the Federation of Swedish Industries, Bert-Olof Svanholm, the Swedish government has chosen a path of "ecological fundamentalism" *(Dagens Nyheter,* February 27th 1997). In Svanholm's view, the attempt of the government to create jobs through an increased share of biofuels is characterised by an anti-technological and regressive spirit: "It is as if one wants to build roads with the help of spades instead of excavators, only to keep people working."

Obviously, the government has not managed to convince Swedish industry with its proposals to rebuild Sweden. While the issue of nuclear energy probably to a large extent contributed to the lack of consensus about a sustainable development, different opinions about economic policy seem to underlie the conflict between government and industry. According to critics, the social-democratic policy - with large-scale state measures and an expansive short-term employment policy - lacks a comprehensive long-term strategy, and is simply a return to the good old days of the Swedish model, when the statey supported massive infrastructural projects of "social engineering" in construction, housing, transporation and energy. The argument is that such approaches are no longer relevant, and that the new plans will not be successfully implemented.

6. Conclusions

In many respects, the efforts to transform Sweden into more sustainable dire tions seem to be constrained by the legacy of the past. The first wave of environmental science and technology policy brought into being a system of end-of-pipe competence integrated into Swedish industry that has tended to dominate both the theory and practice of environmental engineering ever since. Similarly, the major efforts in the 1970s devoted to energy research and development and energy systems analysis meant that the new ideas about environmental management, accounting, and assessment have been primarily appropriated to the energy "sector". The sector-specific competence has been difficult to transform into a more general expertise, or even a more general interest in Swedish industry in pollution prevention, cleaner technologies, or sustainable development. The new approaches have had some influence in the bureaucratic culture, and within the academic culture, as well, but they have made relatively little inroads into the economic policy culture, which has continued to benefit from nuclear energy and the resultant comparatively low energy prices. The fragmented orientation of Swedish (environmental) R&D policy has meant that environmental issues have had difficulty leaving their sectorial isolation and entering into broader discourses about industrial and economic development. But, of course, the problem also has to do with the structure and emphases of Swedish industry. The large corporations that were built up in the late 19th century were based, to a large extent, on the exploitation of natural resources in the mines and the forests, and environmental consequences and impacts were evaluated accordingly. It has proved difficult to restructure Swedish industry and to incorporate an environmental concern into the characteristic forms of economic activity. In this regard, it will be important, in our future research, to explore the ways in which national historical legacies influence contemporary policy-making.

The comparatively high degree of political polarization around environmental issues, and especially around nuclear energy, has also affected the development of environmental science and technology policy in Sweden. Somewhat more than in other countries, "green" concerns and ideas have been given an anti-modernist connotation, and there has been a kind of anti-environmentalist backlash from economists and business leaders that has drawn on ideas from the United States, which have been somewhat less widespread in other European countries.

The strength of Sweden's style, and the success of the national experience, has been in quickly generating new forms of expertise. The main weakness is that the expertise that has been generated, compared to other countries, is often overly specialized and circumscribed, and has been somewhat difficult to integrate with other areas of science and technology. At the same time, because of a tradition of centralized planning and social engineering, as well as of "corporativist" decision-making, it has not been easy for lay people, or public interest organizations, to involve themselves in the policy making process. The hierarchical nature of policy making has obviously played a role; but even more important has been the relatively traditional nature of higher education and research. Compared to other countries, Sweden has largely failed to bring about institutional innovations in environmental science and technology, and environmental education. As we continue with our project, it will be extremely important to try to understand where these barriers to innovation have come from, and why they appear to remain so influential.

References

Berggren, Niclas (1997) *Teskedsjobben - en kritisk granskning av idéerna om "gröna jobb"*. Stockholm: Timbro

Christiansen, Peter Munk, ed (1996) *Governing the Environment: Politics, Policy and Organization in the Nordic Countries*. Nordic Council of Ministers

Elzinga, Aant (1993) "Research and Higher Education in Sweden," in S Rothblatt and B Wittrock, eds, *The European and American University since 1800: historical and sociological essays*. Cambridge University Press

Delegation for Support of Environmentally-adapted Technology (1996) *Strategi för Delegationen för främjande av miljöanpassad teknik*. Stockholm: Ministry of Economic Affairs

Eyerman, Ron et al, eds (1987) *Intellectuals, Universities and the State in Modern Western Societies*. University of California Press

Forskning och samhälle (1996) Regeringens proposition 1996/97:5

Jamison, Andrew (1973) "Science as Control: Environmental Research in Sweden," in *Nordisk Forum*, nr 2, pp 103-117

Jamison, Andrew (1982) *National Components of Scientific Knowledge*. Research Policy Institute

Jamison, Andrew et al (1990) *The Making of the New Environmental Consciousness*. Edinburgh University Press

Jamison, Andrew (1991) "National Styles in Technology Policy. Comparing the Swedish and Danish State Programmes in Microelectronics/Information Technology," in U Hilpert, ed, *State Policies and Techno-Industrial Innovation*, Routledge

Lidskog, Rolf (1996) "Miljöfrågans uppgång - och fall? Kritiska synpunkter på kretsloppsanpassad utveckling, grön produktion och global miljöpolitik," in *Nordisk Samhällsgeografisk Tidskrift*, nr 22, pp 3-25

Lundqvist, Lennart (1971) *Miljövårdsförvaltning och politisk struktur.* Prisma

Lundqvist, Lennart (1996) "Miljörörelsen utestängs", in *Dagens Nyheter*, Sept 2, 1996

Ministry of Economic Affairs (1997) *En uthållig energiförsörjning.* Stockholm

Söderqvist, Thomas (1986) *The Ecologists.* Almqvist and Wiksell

Worster, Donald (1977) *Nature's Economy.* Sierra Club Books

Environmental Technology Policy in a Consensus Mode:
The Case of Denmark

by Erik Baark

1. Introduction

The Danish approach to environmental policy and the promotion of technological innovation aimed at providing solutions to environmental challenges has been designated, by one foreign observer, as "embedded in dialogue mechanisms which included industry and environmental groups, other citizen's groups and independent experts" (Wallace 1995: 42). Indeed, the way that Danes have gone about regulating the environment is frequently portrayed as a result of a particular Danish penchant for decentralized administration (Andersen 1995: 4), a widespread public opinion and a majority of Danish voters which attach high priority to environmental protection, and an industry which is "generally receptive to environmental requirements" (Moe 1995: 30).

While these characterizations may overstate harmonious relationships between the various interest groups involved in environmental policy in Denmark, they nevertheless reflect a basic recognition of the influence of consensus-building in Denmark's political system. As in many other areas of social and political life, environmental policy has been based on a participatory democratic tradition of bringing various stakeholders or interest groups together in order to reach consensus and advise the responsible governmental authorities. All interested parties are assumed to have a legitimate right to negotiation, and to take part in decision-making, and this has been used both for raising issues, as well as for restructuring institutions and administrative procedures. The environmental debate in Denmark has been generally free from the political polarizations that have affected many other European countries; almost all major decisions have been widely agreed upon in parliament by parties representing (almost) the entire political spectrum. But the consensus has often been reached at a high level of generality that has left the specifics to the authoritative bodies, where the forms of public participation have been much more diverse and the nature of participation much more complicated.

This paper will explore the Danish experience as a series of attempts to resolve the tensions between various policy cultures, or key actors in policy making (cf. Jamison and Baark 1990). The specific "national style" of policy making in Denmark that has acted to resolve some of these tensions remains an important factor today, and still provides the main basis for understanding the modalities of public participation in environmental science and technology policy. Increasingly, however, the scope for (nationally) autonomous policy making in the area of environmental issues tends to be circumscribed by international linkages - in particular, by Danish membership in the European Union.

2. The Danish Style of Policy Making

Four aspects of the Danish historical development experience would appear particularly relevant for an understanding of the emergence of a specific style of environmental science and technology policy making in Denmark. They concern 1) the identification of knowledge interests that served to focus attention of scientists and engineers on particular aspects of science and technology; 2) the economic development experience which built on conditions of scarce and vulnerable natural resources; 3) the peaceful transition to a modern parliamentary system in the nineteenth century that was accompanied by a strengthening of local institutions and public debate; and 4) the predominance of international and global ties in an open economy.

During the nineteenth century, the natural sciences in Denmark came to define their principal knowledge interests from a combination of romanticism and empiricism with practically oriented commercial pursuits. There was an emphasis on experimental methods and ideals in science which were connected to the search for the "spirit" in nature, to which was added a philosophical humanism inspired by Søren Kierkegaard. Together these scientific predilections combined with strong traditions for commercial activities which had flourished during the era of the Napoleonic wars to form a particular Danish style in science and technology (Jamison 1982). In some respects, this style synthesized various European influences - British mechanical technologies, German nature philosophies, and French institutions for technical education - to support a rapid process of industrialization in the late nineteenth century.

The expansion of engineering and technical education in Denmark, under the leadership of H.C. Ørsted, provided a source of technical manpower which was crucial for the rapid buildup of technological capabilities and the assimilation of British technology during the 1860s. The educational system was heavily influenced by French and German institutions, and during the early part of the twentieth century was supplemented with a system of vocational training which provided the industry with a highly skilled manpower.

Another particularly influential component of the Danish educational system was the system of the Folk High Schools which sought to provide people with qualifications that went beyond pure training in literary or technical skills, namely, to endow the students with the ability to discuss major social or cultural issues and contribute to society's development through a more active humanism. The philosophy of the poet and priest N.S.F. Grundtvig became a cornerstone of the movement to create folk high schools; his views has been characterized by a foreign observer as "the foundation for a profound cultural synthesis that spoke eloquently to the question of nationalism and national identity" (Borish 1991: 17). The ambition was that these schools would give dignity to the life of the farmer and awaken rural people to the love of learning that would continue long after a student had finished the formal course of study. At the same time, the schools came to represent a unique expression of the social history and that national character of the Danish people, and their role in mobilizing the farming community in the Danish path to modernization should not be underestimated.

Attitudes to nature among Danish scientists and in the public at large were, to a certain degree, shaped by the preponderance of agriculture and the particular ecology of the Danish landscape. Few areas in Denmark have been left untouched by human intervention, and apart from the significant exception of Greenland, wilderness hardly exists. A major ecological crisis appeared during the nineteenth century, when the erosion following the disappearance of forest cover (wood was used extensively for shipbuilding and for fuel) threatened large areas of Danish agricultural land - particularly in Jutland. The efforts to combat this crisis with reforestation and by means of conservation of existing forest resources resulted in a number of institutions including the Danish Heath Society (*Det Danske Hedeselskab*) established in 1866 that mobilized state funds and the population in the fight against land erosion in Jutland.

Economic development in Denmark since the nineteenth century also represents a somewhat unique experience. Endowed with few natural resources or minerals compared to the European nations which started industrialization at the time, Denmark built its economic prosperity primarily on exports of agricultural or agro-industrial products (see, e.g., Senghaas 1982). Probably the most well-known example of this is the successful establishment of a dairy industry based on the cooperative movement, which in turn proved important for a whole system of technological innovation (Edquist and Lundvall, 1993; Lundvall 1992). As late as the late 1950s, almost two-thirds of Danish commodity exports derived from agriculture or food-processing industries. For this reason, the interests of producers in agriculture or the agro-industrial sector have had a major say in Danish politics, including an established relation to the Liberal Party (*Venstre*) which has continued to be one of the largest political parties in the Danish parliament.

Denmark's industrialization subsequently took the form of a process that relied on a large number of small or medium-sized enterprises with a highly skilled work force, and which grew on the basis of rapid diffusion and adaptation of technology, mostly imported from countries with major research and development activities. Danish industry includes very few large firms and for more than a century, the Danish state has followed a laissez-faire policy with regard to industrial development, leaving the initiative primarily to private industry and minimizing the role of public enterprises. Consequently, industry and business has tended to constitute a relatively autonomous body of interests and, in spite of the link which exists between the Federation of Danish Industries and the Conservative Party *(Konservative Folkeparti)*, these interests have seldom been allowed to occupy a strong power base in the Danish political landscape.

The democratic traditions have had a long period of formation in Danish history, and Denmark was one of the few countries in Europe that accomplished a peaceful transition to the parliamentary system. The mobilization of farmers by the Liberal Party (*Venstre*) in the late nineteenth century created a viable opposition to the political dominance of the landowner's Right Party (*Høire*), which increasingly came to represent the new class of industrialists based in Copenhagen. The strength of the liberals and, during the early part of the twentieth century, of the Social Democrats led to a distinct tradition for delegation of administrative tasks to regional or local government. Combined with the cooperative movement that relied on local entrepreneurship and the educational institutions associated with the Folk High Schools, which aimed to enhance both the practical skills of young people in the countryside and their ability to understand and participate in debates over major political issues, the Danish tradition for decentralized administration has occupied a core position in setting the stage for public debates and policy making related to environmental science and technology.

Given the position of Denmark at the midpoint of maritime trade in the Baltic and the North Sea, and with the significance of agricultural exports, the Danish economy has continued to be strongly integrated in the international market. The open economy has also been accompanied by a receptiveness toward the cultural and social influence of the large European neighbours, e.g. France, Germany and later Britain. In many ways, borrowing from such European cultures became an important element of the way in which the Danish culture became a hybrid of Scandinavian traditions and the new stimuli which came to Denmark from other areas in Europe. Many institutions in Denmark relied on access to international sources of knowledge and skills; for example, universities encouraged students to study abroad and for long periods the certification of a master carpenter would require that the apprentice had obtained a journeyman's certificate after working abroad.

These four aspects provided a fertile ground for the development of an approach to environmental science and technology policy that has been unique in some respects, but also similar to international experience in other respects. Probably the combination of romantic and still pragmatic knowledge interests of the Danish scientific community with an economic and political system mobilizing the local communities in the development of the country proved very useful in exploiting existing technology under new organizational patterns. During the first half of the twentieth century, a new element of "dialogue" was added to this structure, as a framework for conflict resolution grew out of the labour struggles that culminated around the turn of the century. Since the Social Democrats succeeded in marshalling all the major political parties, the labour movement and the employers' organization in an effort to weather the economic crisis of the 1930s, the basis of a corporatist relationship was established that came to define much of the political context of the welfare state in the post-war period.

3. From Conservation to Environmentalism

Given the ecological problems that Denmark had experienced in the nineteenth century and the role of an active local and governmental policy to alleviate the consequences of the deforestation, there was a reasonably vital tradition for conservation at the turn of the century. This tradition gave rise to the first - and still one of the dominant - popular organizations engaged in the promotion of environmental protection. The Danish Society for the Conservation of Nature (*Danmarks Naturfredningsforening*) was established in 1911 and soon mobilized local citizens together with a range of concerned scientists in the work to protect natural areas which were considered of particular aesthetic, scientific, or recreational value. During the 1930s, the Society for the Conservation of Nature was charged with the responsibility to initiate and manage proposals for the preservation of sites and landscapes. The delegation of such responsibility for implementation of a conservation policy to a private organization was, to a large degree, a result of the decentralized and corporatist approach to policy making and implementation in Denmark.

The influence of the Society of Nature Conservation therefore became more influential (and, perhaps, more established) in Denmark than in many other countries, and many have come to regard the organization almost as a kind of public institution. Some of the concerned scientists who have been involved in the society have been members of governmental advisory committees and continue to play an important role in policy making (Andersen 1995: 6-7). Nevertheless, the society suffered a major setback in 1963, when a new set of laws aiming at the protection of land (*jordlov*) was defeated in a referendum. Partly due to this political defeat, the society did not become actively engaged in the debate on pollution when it started to take shape in the 1960s. Another organization which has existed for many years is the Anglers' Association (*Danmarks Sportsfiskerforbund*) established in 1938, which has created an awareness of the need to protect waterways and which has conducted a continuous lobbying of national and local authorities.

Altogether, the Danish policy discourse on environmental issues, such as it was, prior to the late 1960s was dominated by these organizations. The central and local governmental authorities had responsibility for environmental protection, but, until the late 1960s, the environment was not an area of high political priority. The measures that were taken were primarily focused in technical improvements, in waste water treatment and nature protection. Although there was some public involvement in relation to conservation issues - which areas to preserve, etc - the overall approach was primarily technically oriented and relied on forms of expertise, mainly located at the universities and at some of the research institutes, under the Academy of Technological Sciences, which was founded in 1938.

The growing awareness of environmental problems in the late 1960s derived primarily from two very different sources. On the one hand, some of the literature which was published abroad - particularly in the United States - on the emerging environmental "crisis" and the effects of industrial pollution on nature and human health was translated into Danish and widely referred to in the media. On the other hand, a certain social movement "sector" of the civil society that had been involved in the peace movement and demonstrations against atomic bombs in the 1950s was increasingly turning its attention to national affairs, and gradually coming to focus on the effects of industrial production, consumerism and affluence on the environment.

The issues lay dormant in the political debate, however, until they became associated more directly with the alternative political ideologies that grew out of the youth rebellion and the student movement of the late 1960s (Jamison et al 1990). The most important organization in this connection was NOAH, started in 1969 by biology and architecture students in Copenhagen, which soon developed into a national organization of environmental activism. NOAH utilized scientific information and cooperated with scientists who themselves sympathised with the effort to act as "counter-experts" particularly in relation to the media. In this way, the first efforts at creating public awareness of the environmental problems in Denmark were carried out by an alliance between students and the media that was highly critical of the "establishment" - which was depicted as a combination of apathetic governmental institutions, profiteering business interests, and a disengaged, problematic scientific expert community.

The activist approach of NOAH and other radical groups that emerged in the late 1960s was grounded in a long-standing Danish tradition for local debate and participatory democracy - associated with the cooperative movement and the so-called Folk High Schools, that were established in the 19th century as part of a rural populism that opposed the new industrial urban bourgeoisie in the cities. As in other countries, the new social movements, like NOAH, that emerged in the 1960s created a new civic policy culture for environmental science and technology that was to grow stronger over the following decade.

4. Institutionalization and Sectorization

One of the first concrete results of the attention to environmental issues which, for instance, the campaigns of NOAH created in Denmark was that the government established a Danish Pollution Council in 1969. This institution, which was charged with the task of examining the level of scientific knowledge related to the environmental issues and to prepare the ground for an environmental policy, was abolished in 1971, shortly after the government had named a Minister of Pollution Control.

A particularly important source of inspiration in Denmark was the United Nations Conference on the Human Environment in Stockholm in the summer of 1972. The conference provided for many European countries a significant indication that the international community was beginning to recognize the seriousness of environmental problems, and that new kinds of policy bodies and laws were required. Thus, in Denmark, the 1970s witnessed the creation of an institutional structure to deal with environmental and pollution problems, first at the national level and later in the local administration throughout Denmark. The main body for environmental policy within the national government apparatus has been the Danish Environmental Protection Agency (EPA) established in 1972. One year after its establishment, this agency was in 1973 brought under a new Ministry of the Environment which has existed within the Danish Government until it was merged with the Ministry of Energy in 1994 (Moe 1995: 45-48). From the beginning, the EPA sought to involve various interest groups in society in the process of policy-making and legislation, entering, in particular, into a dialogue with the Confederation of Danish Industries (at the time called Industrirådet, now named Dansk Industri). What was significant about the Danish system was that the ministry was given responsibility for several other agencies - for physical planning, forestry and nature protection - as well as air pollution, water pollution, and waste. Research institutions were also established under the ministry, most important being the Danish Environment Research Institute and the Danish Geological Research Institute. The fact that environmental issues were thus given ministerial status, and that a range of different activities were all placed under a single ministry has meant that environmental policy in Denmark has been somewhat stronger in relation to other policy areas. It has also meant that there has, from the early 1970s, been a strong "elitist" and bureaucratic tone to policy making. The special style of "ministerial rule" has also meant that the role of the parliament has been relatively weak in Denmark: decision-making has been delegated to the ministry.

While, on the one hand, the 1970s thus became a period of initial dialogue between government and business that was to have considerable repercussions for the formulation and implementation of environmental policies (cf. Wallace 1995), it was also a decade of an increasing professional and administrative dominance over the political agenda related to the environment. In this sense, Denmark witnessed a process of sectorization (or bureaucratization) of environmental issues in the 1970s which was quite parallel to what was taking place in other countries (cf. Jamison 1996). The legal framework for pollution control and environmental administration was also imported more or less directly from Sweden. With the extension of an administrative network and the expansion of the group of people who were working professionally with environmental issues came a more explicit expression of a bureaucratic policy culture.

The public debate on environmental issues did not, however, disappear on account of the new political and administrative initiatives. In contrast, it became even more important as it became associated with the energy crisis and the search for alternative means of energy supply. More specifically, the debate concerning nuclear energy, an option that was gradually abandoned by the Danish government in the late 1970s, provided a framework for the Organization for Information about Nuclear Power (OOA) to develop from the basis of the environmental activism of NOAH into social movements aiming to mobilize the "grass roots". In addition, the popular debate on alternative energy sources and various public awareness and information campaigns, encouraged social movements to generate local debate and practical initiatives which gradually became an established mode of public participation in the political decision-making in Denmark (Læssøe 1995: 39-40).

It is also likely that the experience of the 1970s left a significant legacy of environmental awareness and concern among major political parties. When an initiative was taken to form a Green Party in 1983, this legacy made it difficult for the new party to gain a sufficient following at the elections for the Parliament. Other parties such as the People's Socialist Party (*Socialistisk Folkeparti*) and the Social Liberals (*Radikale Venstre*) have developed an explicit profile regarding environmental policies, and there has been a gradual "greening" of nearly all the political parties during the 1980s (Andersen 1995: 12)

The institutionalization of the environmental administration in Denmark was the delegation of responsibility of much of the environmental policies and regulation to local authorities in the counties and municipalities (Moe 1995: 52-57). As part of the implementation of the Environmental Protection Act of 1973, the county administrations were made responsible for undertaking projects related to the cleaning of waste-water, and for issuing environmental consents to the most troublesome industrial enterprises. While the delegation of such responsibilities to the counties has succeeded in gradually creating a higher level of technical and legal competence for environmental regulation at the lower levels of the Danish society, the same system has been criticised for inefficiency and the potential collusion of interests between regulators and offenders at the local level (Georg 1994).

5. Commercialization and the Making of a Technology Policy for the Environment

One of the problems that became clearer as Denmark moved into the 1980s was that the attempts made so far to solve environmental problems tended to seek pollution abatement by means of end-of-pipe solutions, and that new approaches stressing a change in productive technology were far more effective. This realization came also with the experience of energy-saving experiments and pro-active policies that had become an integral component of Danish energy policy and administration in the 1970s.

Given the perceived limitations of supply of energy sources - further reinforced by the decision to aboandon a nuclear power programme - the

Danish government had emphasized the need to resolve the energy crisis by saving energy and encouraging the transition to renewable energy sources. This led, on the one hand, to the establishment and rapid growth of the Danish wind turbine industry which had been reasonably successful in showing the feasibility of advanced systems for generation of renewable energy to supplement traditional sources, and which has been very successful in exporting technologies to other countries. On the other hand, the regulatory framework in the energy sector came to stress the use of various legal and economic instruments to encourage more energy-efficient technologies in industries as diverse as energy production, building construction, and consumer products. The attention gradually shifted towards identification of solutions to the environmental problems that could be integrated earlier on in the cycles of production and consumption. The relative effectiveness of economic incentives and penalties in improving the technological and organizational capacity for saving energy could inspire similar initiatives in the environmental field: a move from end-of-pipe solutions to a model that emphasizes preventive solutions including the development and diffusion of cleaner technology. Beginning in 1986, the Danish government has launched a series of major support programs in cleaner technology. Compared to most other European countries, the Danish efforts have been substantial, and have spread the various preventive technical approaches to environmental problems throughout the Danish industry.

In the first phase, from 1986-1989, the effort was concentrated primarily on investigating the potential for cleaner technologies in different branches of the economy, and in conducting demonstration projects in particular firms. The general approach followed similar "national programs" in technology development that had taken place in the 1980s, in relation to information technology and biotechnology, and were based on the long-standing Danish emphasis in technology policy on demonstration projects.

The second phase of the cleaner technology program, from 1990-92 involved a more active broadening of focus, as well as increased competence-building and information dissemination. Courses were held at engineering colleges and associations, handbooks were written, and special branch consulting schemes in cleaner technology were established in four particular branches: furniture-making, meat processing, fish production, and metal-working. At the same time, environmental management systems were instituted in a number of small and medium-sized companies with governmental support, and major efforts were taken to document the experiences with cleaner technology, through a number of technology assessment projects at the technological universities. From 1993, the efforts have expanded further, as the environmental administration has adopted a more flexible, interactive approach, seeking to pass responsibility and policy initiative from the public to the private sector (cf Remmen 1995).

The new attempts to alleviate the problems of environmental degradation were, to a significant extent, funded on the blending of the element of dialogue between public and private interests that has characterized Danish approaches from the beginning, and a new ideology of commercialization and the use of market forces in regulation. In the political atmosphere that prevailed in Denmark during the 1980s, when the government was usually based on a combination of parties from the centre to the right of the political spectrum under the leadership of the Conservative Party, there was a strong leaning towards liberal economic policies and indirect instruments of regulation, i.e., small government. Even in areas where the government was unable to secure a majority of votes in the Parliament for its policies - as the case was for much of the environmental legislation which was dominated by the so-called "green majority" (social liberals, social democrats and two left-wing parties) - the subsequent implementation of policies tended to be framed in the manner of indirect regulation.

The concrete administration of policies related to environmental science and technology were typical of an economic policy culture and paid more attention to ensuring the cooperation of business interests, or even the promotion of such interests for instance in connection with the growth of the environmental consulting engineering firms and the establishment of a competitive industry for the production and exports of wind turbines. In fact, the case of the wind turbine industry in Denmark illustrates the extent to which a combination of innovative policies, local industrial entrepreneurship, and a set of priorities evolving from the political pressure of public debate contributed to the shaping of new technologies (Jørgensen and Karnoe 1995).

This shift in awareness and attention to a wider economic perspective was also reinforced by the initiatives which sought to integrate technology assessment more directly into policy making procedures. In many ways, a particular Danish style of technology assessment found its application in the policy debates related to areas such as biotechnology and cleaner technology.

The public debate on biotechnology in Denmark in the 1980s indicates how conflicts between critics and proponents became mediated by various approaches to technology assessment (Baark and Jamison 1990). In Denmark, the debate on the environmental risks associated with biotechnology had flared up when one of the major pharmaceutical firms planned to erect production facilities for production of insuline using genetically engineered microorganisms, and these plans were opposed by the local community after an awareness campaign conducted by NOAH. There followed a period of intense lobbying at government institutions by both NOAH and the representatives of the industry. In addition, the government sponsored a programme of public information dissemination, local debate meetings in communities all over Denmark, and a series of so-called "Consensus Conferences" relating to safety and ethical aspects of biotechnology; all these activities were seen as components of a type of technology assessment involving public participation and led by the Board of Technology (*Teknologinævnet*) which had been set up by the Danish Parliament. The government finally decided to enact very restrictive legislation regarding genetic manipulation in 1986. Nevertheless, the implementation of this legislation typically facilitated a dialogue with representatives of industry and agriculture, and the requirements for approval of field experiments were relaxed considerably by the Minister of the Environment in 1989. In one sense, the opportunity for public debate and the adoption of stringent legislation served to console fears among the population of the risks associated with biotechnology; simultaneously, the flexibility of implementation in conjunction with a dialogue between the government bodies and the industry ensured that the business remained positive to undertaking safety measures.

The emergence of constructive technology assessment as a significant new concept in Denmark has also been influential in the promotion of cleaner technology (cf. Remmen, 1994). The point is that constructive technology assessment has evolved methodologies for the identification of areas of public concern, priorities for action related to the development and diffusion of new technology and, in particular, proposed means to assist policy makers in ensuring that desireable technologies become adopted in industries or agriculture. Several cases in Denmark have illustrated that a constructive technology assessment can encourage patterns of "dynamic regulation" that extends beyond the administration of compliance to environmental standards and instead promotes the drawing up of environmental action plans jointly by firms and local or national authorities (see, e.g. Remmen and Nielsen 1994).

Simultaneously with the increased popularity of closer public-private interaction in environmental regulation, the 1980s witnessed a transformation of the role and influence of the social movements. The most significant change happened to NOAH, which temporarily faded away as a major actor in the environmental debate, with the action related to biotechnology safety being one of the last major cases of significant influence based on the mobilization of public interest. Instead, the role of promoters of alternative environmental perspectives and dissemination of information was gradually taken over by more professionalized non-governmental organizations such as Greenpeace and the World Wildlife Fund, which also had a definitely more international outlook. In the 1990s, however, NOAH has been actively involved in the new international efforts in environmental technology as well as in the discourse on "environmental carrying capacity".

Actually, there was a transition from a primarily national environmental debate in Denmark in the 1980s to a debate that more explicitly recognized regional and global perspectives. This internationalization of the debate and policy initiatives was motivated by a number of important events, one of which was the Tjernobyl nuclear accident which quickly brought home to many people the significance of environmental degradation or disasters in neighbouring countries. The realization that SO_2 emissions were responsible for destruction of forests with acid rain added to a sense of inter-connectedness, and in that case Denmark was also a culprit since Danish SO_2 emissions carried with the wind were contributing to environmental degradation in Sweden.

A second factor was the debate that was raised in connection with the preparation and publication of the report of the Brundtland Commission; here again was strong argument for attention being paid to the international repercussions of the environmental policies pursued by other countries - repercussions which were seen as potentially having direct effects on the Danish environment. In addition, the perspective of the developing countries which was reflected in the Brundtland report appealed to the Danish public where the large majority of the population has consistently supported Danish development assistance.

But probably the most important component in the transition to a more international perspective in environmental science and technology policy was the fact that European integration through the work of the EEC, and later the European Union (EU), became a much more concrete item on the Danish political agenda in the late 1980s. During the first fifteen years of Denmark's membership in the EU until 1987, the European Commission drew up a range of directives which sought to define some general rules for environmental administration - e.g. requirements for Environmental Impact Assessment - or responded to specific incidents related to the environment such as the Seveso accident (Moe 1995: 35-36). Few directives would affect Danish legislation or administration directly since the European political bodies did not have the power to intervene directly in national policies. After the Single European Act came into force in 1987, however, the Commission used the harmonization provision in an attempt to ensure a common standard for environmental regulation and administration in the member countries. This tendency to grant the EU greater powers in harmonizing environmental policies and administration was further reinforced with the Maastricht Treaty that entered into force in 1993.

Overall, the 1980s came to represent the dominance of the economic policy culture; for example, levies on CFC and energy utilization was introduced to encourage more efficient production methods, and waste and packaging taxes also served preventive purposes. In addition, some of the revenues from environmental taxes gradually became significant contributions to the state budget (cf. Andersen 1994; Andersen 1995: 17). The use of economic instruments in environmental regulation, which was providing a regular source of income based on taxes and levies, was thus important for the growing power of the EPA during a period where the budgets of the state administration were generally reduced. But the primary motivation behind the adoption of such instruments was probably the perceived failure of bureaucratic approaches to regulation and, simultaneously, a new popularity of neo-classical models of the behaviour of economic agents. The popularity of such approaches notwithstanding, they have proved difficult to pursue in Denmark without complementary initiatives of a more traditional regulatory character (cf. Georg 1993).

6. Conclusions: Toward Integration and Internationalization

It has been probably the widespread apprehensions among the Danish voters regarding the ability of the European Union to ensure an adequate level of environmental protection that contributed to the defeat at a referendum in 1992 of the Danish Parliament's majority vote to join the EU under the conditions of the Maastricht Treaty. A referendum the following year approved a new proposal of the Parliament based on the Edinburgh agreement - so that Denmark could join the EU under the Maastricht Treaty. One of the significant concessions obtained by the Danish government with the Edinburgh agreement concerned precisely the authority of the Danish government to maintain higher levels of environmental standards than more hesitant member states or the EU directives which often represent a compromise. In other words, the European influence in the Danish environmental policy remains important and a often cause of controversy in political debates in Denmark.

But tensions between various national actors related to environmental science and technology policy have not entirely subsided, and there are still areas where conflicts flare up between social activists, government institutions and vested interests in society. A notable example is that of the policies aimed at alleviating the environmental impact of agriculture. In 1973 the Agricultural Council had successfully resisted environmental regulation, and this sector maintained a special position since the concept of pollution did not include normal agricultural practises. In 1982, some consideration of the environmental impact was introduced into a new Watercourse Act, but a subsequent attempt to revise this in 1991 nearly failed due to the resistance of the farmers. These initiatives were based on the new framework for environmental policies which now included effluents from agriculture, and not merely industrial pollution as it had been the case in the 1970s and 1980s. The existence of nitrogen leaching from agricultural land, the seriousness of which became recognized in 1984, and the subsequent discovery of serious oxygen depletion in Danish marine waters in 1986 led to a public debate where, for instance, the Society for the Conservation of Nature became very influential in designing a new policy. The Danish Parliament subsequently passed an Action Plan on the Aquatic Environment in 1987, which demanded that agricultural discharges were to be reduced by 50%, much to the chagrin of the representatives of the farmer's lobby (see Røjel 1990).

Another important area of conflict arose with the perceived need to follow up on the Danish commitments to international meetings such as the Rio Conference in 1992 and the Montreal Protocol. The Danish industry had serious apprehensions about government initiatives to reduce the emission of hazardous substances such as CFCs or CO_2, particularly since these initiatives tended to be viewed as excessive in comparison with similar efforts in other European countries. The CO_2 levy was introduced in 1993 and increased in 1996; together with the energy levy, it is designed to further encourage the diffusion of energy effective technologies in Danish enterprises. To a considerable extent such conflicting interests emerged between the government and industry representatives, while both the media and environmental organizations were showing little independent initiative.

In contrast, the Brent Spar incident in 1995, where a Greenpeace action developed into a boycott of Shell by a large number of consumers and business firms in Denmark, proved that the media and activist organizations such as Greenpeace could still mobilize considerable resistance in relation to environmental issues. Particularly noteworthy in connection with this action is the phenomenon that consumer behaviour is becoming increasingly influential in relation to environmental issues. Another aspect of this phenomenon is that the growing market for products from ecological agriculture in Denmark has been fostered by a new demand among consumers who are willing to pay higher prices for products that are certified to meet particular standards. To a certain extent, the new role of consumers demonstrate that the market forces are gaining importance as a way to regulate the economy.

One of the most important aspects of the Danish environmental science and technology policy in the 1990s were the efforts to ensure integration of policy initiatives - i.e., to move beyond the sectoral perception of the environmental problems and ensure that areas such as energy, transport, agriculture and industry would integrate environmental concerns in their work. The actual policy making and administration is still split up according to sectoral responsibilities of ministries, but the Ministry of the

Environment and Energy is attempting to provide overall coordination of the activities in each sector. In the nineties environmental policy have been modernized. The modernization is primarily linked to integration of the pollution prevention and precautionary principles into the existing environmental policy, meaning that the environmental requirements for industry must be based on "best available" technology, or BAT (cf. Nielsen, 1996). The modernization also involves the introduction of new market-based policy instruments, such as agreements, sustainable public procurement, ecolabelling, product-oriented environmental policy, green taxes, etc.

The process of policy integration and cooperation among major actors has been evident in the effort to promote cleaner technology. One the one hand, the government initiated a programme of support for cleaner technologies, attempting to reduce the costs of complying with existing emission standards and achieving future standards for emission of, e.g., heavy metals. On the other hand, the EPA has become increasingly forthcoming in entering into active dialogues with individual firms to find solutions to their problems. In many cases, the new approach to interaction between business and public authorities has also been associated with the methodology of Life Cycle Analysis (LCA) or "cradle-to-grave" analysis for products. In the case of LCA, for instance, business firms have sought to develop a better environmental image for their products by examining the "environmental load" of each of the components that enters into the production process; frequently they have discovered that there were substantial cost savings associated with "greener" production methods and naturally this has created a substantial amount of good-will among business interests.

The Danish experiences in cleaner technology and environmental management have also become important elements of development assistance. Major programs have been initiated to export cleaner technologies and environmental management competence to developing countries and to countries in central and eastern Europe. As the Stockholm conference in 1972 had earlier been important in the institutionalization of environmental policy in Denmark, the 1992 United Nations conference in Brazil on environment and development also had a big impact on Danish policy making. Denmark is one of the most active promulgators of the Agenda 21, and there are a wide range of local activities that are coordinated through the Ministry of the Environment. There have also been major new programs in environment and development, initiated both by Danida, the Danish Agency for Development Assistance, and by the Environmental Protection Agency, aimed at linking environmental concern more closely into technology transfer projects.

References

Andersen, Mikael Skou (1994) *Governance by Green Taxes: Making Pollution Prevention Pay* Manchester: Manchester University Press

Andersen, Mikael Skou (1995), "Conflict and Compromise in Environmental policy: Capacity Building in Denmark", paper forthcoming in Martin Jäniche and Helmut Weidner, eds, *National Environmental Policies - A Comparative Study of Capacity Building* Berlin: Springer Verlag

Baark, Erik and Andrew Jamison (1990), "Biotechnology and Culture: The Impact of Public Debates on Government Regulation in the United States and Denmark" *Technology in Society,* No. 12, pp. 27-44.

Borish, Steven M. (1991). *The Land to the Living: The Danish Folk High Schools and Denmark's Non-violent Path to Modernization* Nevada City, California: Blue Dolphin Publishing

Edquist, Charles and Bengt-Åke Lundvall (1993), "Comparing the Danish and Swedish Systems of Innovation" in Richard R. Nelson, *National Innovation Systems: A Comparative Analysis* Oxford: Oxford University Press

Georg, Susse (1993). *Når løsningen bliver problemet - miljøregulering i økonomisk perspektiv* [When the solution becomes the problem - Environmental regulation in an economic perspective] Copenhagen: Samfundslitteratur

Georg, Susse (1994). "Regulating the Environment: Changing from Constraint to Gentle Coercion" *Business Strategy and the Environment*

Jamison, Andrew (1982). *National Components of Scientific Knowledge: A Contribution to the Social Theory of Science*, Lund: Research Policy Institute

Jamison, Andrew (1996) "The Shaping of the Global Environmental Agenda" in S. Lash et al. (eds) *Risk, Environment Modernity* London: Sage Publishers

Jamison, Andrew, Ron Eyerman, Jaqueline Cramer with Jeppe Læssøe (1990). *The Making of the New Environmental Consciousness: A Comparative Study of the Environmental Movements in Sweden, Denmark and the Netherlands* Edinburgh: Edinburgh University Press

Læssøe, Jeppe (1995). Folkeoplysning - en vej til miljøansvarlig handlen? (Arbejdsrapport fra Miljøstyrelsen, No. 2, 1995) Copenhagen: Miljøstyrelsen

Lundvall, Bengt-Åke (1992) *National Systems of Innovation - Towards a Theory of Innovation and Interactive Learning* London. Pinter Publishers

Moe, Mogens (1996). Environmental Administration in Denmark, (Environment News, No. 17) Copenhagen: Ministry of Environment and Energy, Danish Environmental Protection Agency

Remmen, Arne (1994). "Pollution Prevention, Cleaner Technologies and Industry" in Arie Rip, Tom Misa and Johan Schot (eds.). Managing Technology in Society London: Pinter Press

Remmen, Arne and Eskild H. Nielsen (1994). "New Incentives for Pollution Prevention: Environmental Strategies for Companies and Public Regulation" Paper presented at the Third International IACT Conference on Policies and Incentives for Clean Technology, 6-8 April 1994, Vienna, Austria.

Røjel, Jørgen (1990) *Fra Anarki til Hysteri: Dansk Miljøpolitik 1960-90* [From Anarchy to Hysteria: Danish Environmental Policy 1960-90] Copenhagen: Samleren

Senghaas, Dieter (1982). *Von Europa Lernen: Entwicklungs- geshiichtliche Betrachtungen* Frankfurt am Main: Suhrkamp

Wallace, David (1995). *Environmental Policy and Industrial Innovation: Strategies in Europe, the USA and Japan* (The Royal Institute of International Affairs. Energy and Environmental Programme), London: Earthscan Publications

Environmental Science and Technology Policy In Norway

by Per Østby

1. Introduction

Since 1960 important changes have taken place in Norwegian society. While the 1960s were a time of optimism and widespread belief in social and economic progress linked to modern science and technology, the following decades saw this optimism reduced substantially. A main reason for this change was the increasing focus on environmental problems. One side of these problems was the identification of industrial pollution and the over-exploitation of natural resources. Another reason was a changing conception of hazards and dangers. What earlier had been regarded as acceptable, now became intolerable risks. A third reason was the development of new policies to identify, control or solve these tensions.

Related to all three matters, science and expertise had a key position. But even if experts and scientists were the central actors, problem definitions and policy formulation have been reshaped, modified or reinterpreted by other actors in industry and administration. Civil society has also had influence at different levels and with varying degrees of success.

The different views and the various remedies or policies proposed to control "the problems" have seemed to form phase-dependent "problem-fields"; the first phase being the time from the late 1950s to 1970. The second phase, the years from 1970 to 1983, was a time of "institution-building", with the establishment of the Ministry of the Environment as the most important event. From 1983 onwards, there has been a kind of regrouping of organisations and institutions, often described in terms such as ecological modernisation.

My main intention in this article is to describe the constitution, integration and reconstruction of the environment problematic, in the time from 1960 to present. I focus on the relation between what is often seen as two different processes: the public influence and engagement in environmental questions, and the development of a science and technology policy concerning the environment.

2. The Constitution of a New Problem-Field

The time from 1960 to 1970 has been heralded as "The Golden Years". The background for this label was a sound and improving economy both for the state and the general public. Not only the wealthy, but even workers could afford to buy luxury items such as television sets, private cars and cabins in the countryside. Another name put on these years was "Modern Norway", pointing at the rapid transformation of society, industry and trade. A simplified picture shows a policy along two lines:

The first comprises large-scale investment in heavy industry based on extensive use of cheap energy from hydro-power plants. The second is a growing optimism towards the potential outcome of scientific and technologi-cal development. While the spokesmen for the heavy industry paradigm are found among the economic experts in the central administration, the science and technology line was shaped and pushed forward by enthusiastic engineers gradually forming an alliance with modernist entrepreneurs in the same administration. The policy outcome of the first line was *The Plan for*

Northern Norway (NNP), initiated in 1950. *NNP* was meant to be a tool for the modernisation of traditional trades and to bring new industry to what was seen as the backward areas of northern Norway. In 1960, *NNP* was reformulated as a program for less "developed" regions all over Norway. The effects of programs like *NNP* were migration and urbanisation; life and occupations dramatically altered for many people. An attempt was made to implement the second policy line through the establishment of *The Norwegian Council for Science and Technology (NTNF)* in 1946. The *NTNF*'s main objective was to fund and supervise technical-industrial research in Norway. This line resulted in the building up of a comprehensive research institute sector, mainly financed by public money, directed by *NTNF*. Until the early 1960s the funds were largely directed towards research projects related to the military and industry. Gradually *NTNF* also came to initiate and fund applied social research, and from the 1970s until the early 1980s it was the main instrument for environmental research.

In spite of the economic well being and the optimism in science and technology, the 1960s saw the contours of new thoughts emerge concerning the relation between societal and economical development and the situation of the natural and social environment. A diffuse tension was triggered by several contingent factors. The first was a growing awareness concerning the damage to nature. The second was a growing focus on the transformations of traditional occupational and community structures. Thirdly, there were administrative efforts to monitor and regulate natural and societal bottlenecks created by the modernisation process. In addition to these scientific and administrative efforts, a growing number of marginal social groups joined forces with concerned scientists and intellectuals and challenged the existing growth policy.

As early as the 1950s, farmers in Årdal and on Sunndalsøra complained about the smoke from local aluminium plants destroying the vegetation. Some were financially compensated for damages. In addition to this and similar public worries, the international scientific community pointed out the potential dangers and threats caused by the industrialisation and rationalisation process. Rachel Carson's book *Silent Spring* came out in 1962 and Barry Commoner's *Science and Survival* was published in 1966. Georg Borgströms books on the global food crisis also met with great interest in Norway. These and similar publications inspired Norwegian researchers and intellectuals, and *The Biocidecommittee* was initiated by *The Norwegian Association for Zoology* in 1964. Professor Ragnhild Sundby wrote about "global poisoning" in the periodical *Naturen* in 1965 and the biologists Eilif Dahl and Olav Gjærevoll tried to inform the general public about the new dangers produced by the modern industrial society.

In addition to the criticism from researchers in the natural sciences, social scientists and humanists pointed out the tensions caused by the modernisation process in society. In 1966 the sociologist Ottar Brox published *What Is Happening in Northern Norway?*. The book was an attack on the adopted modernisation policy. Brox's criticism developed along two lines. The first was emotional and value-based: according to Brox the *NNP* policy eroded the local communities' traditional ways of living. The second line was linked to the economic rationality of the policy. Was it sure, he asked, that the modernisation policy would lead to economic growth? In the long run, would it not be more economical to keep small units that could combine different types of production and exploit the natural resources? Brox's and similar populist criticism, primarily among those directly affected by the policy, were adopted by others and after some years the populist "movement" became intermingled with political radicalisation, the discussions about local democracy and the new concern for the natural environment. The integration of all these elements, forming a new sector, is exemplified by Hartvig Sætra's book *The Eco-political Socialism* from 1973. Sætra tried to show the connection between the political system, the destruction of nature and possible solutions for changing this development. The key factor came to be "local community", which became synonymous with "the good life".

A second "anti-program" was initiated by Arne Næss, Sigmund Kvaløy and interested intellectuals and students at the Department of Philosophy at the University of Oslo. From 1969 they held debate meetings, leading up to the establishment of the Collaborating Groups for the Protection of Nature and the Environment (*snm*). The philosophy of Arne Næss was a quite important part of the debates and *snm*. Næss pointed out the pollution problem, the unequal distribution of resources, the need to stabilise population growth, the demand for more self-government, local administration, decentralisation. Other elements were more radical, such as his species equality. Næss, with references to Spinoza, suggested a delegation of natural rights from humans to all life. According to Næss all elements of the biosphere had equal rights. Instead of a survival of the fittest, there should be a partnership of species, he claimed. Another peculiar principle was "*Docta ignorantia* - conscious ignorance". Næss also made a distinction between deep ecology and "shallow" ecology. The latter would according to Næss end up in technical reforms. Pollution would be solved by technical solutions instead of attacking the causes of the problem. According to Næss, deep ecology should stick to alternative technologies, technologies devised in harmony with nature (Naess 1972; Naess 1976)..

The attack on centralisation and the emergence of new problems coincided with the growing administrative belief in science and technology as means to map, explain or propose technical solutions to societal problems caused by the modernisation process. The heavy post-war investment in industry and centralisation created societal bottlenecks that could not be ignored by the authorities in the long run. Different policy measures were undertaken to meet these problems. One step was the establishment of research institutes or councils. Under strong protests from industry, a committee on smoke pollution was appointed by Parliament in 1957 and the Air Pollution Council for Concessions to Industry was established in 1961. The power and impact of this council came to be very limited. The ability to both supervise and regulate industrial pollution proved unsatisfactory. One key problem was that the laws for these types of problems were not fit for the new situation. Another was the lack of expertise in handling these matters. An attempt to solve the problem of lack of expertise was made in establishing the Institute for Air Research (*NILU*) in 1969 (Ustvedt 1981: 441 - 443).

While the institutionalisation of research related to air pollution evolved slowly, the Norwegian Institute for Water Research (*NIVA*) was started as early as in 1958. The third field emerged when local and central administrations had to counter existing and anticipated communication problems. A committee for town and city research appointed in 1963 was reorganised as the Institute for Urban and Regional Research (*NIBR*) in 1967. In addition to the build-up of scientific/administrative resources, other administrative policy measures were also tried out. Several governmental commissions were appointed, with the *Modalsliutvalget*, or Modalsli committee, and the Resources Commission as the most important. *Modalsliutvalget*'s mandate was to evaluate the distribution of responsibility between the different ministries. Initially this was an attempt to rationalise the administrative apparatus, in line with the administration's concern about a lack of effectiveness. The commission's work came to influence the integration of environmental concern into the administration in a substantial way, consequently leading to the establishment of *The Ministry of the Environment (MD)*. Such governmental commissions became one way for the general public to have their voices heard in relation to the shaping of administrative and science and technology policies.

A third way of dealing with environmental problems and setting up policy measures is the passing of legislation. New acts were passed in 1954, 1965 and 1970. In 1960, a commission on the laws for clean water was appointed, and in 1970 the law for the protection of water was passed. Possibly most important was the *Planning and Building Act* debated in Parliament in 1965. This act, in line with the work of the *Commission of Resources*, explicitly delineated the distribution of the responsibility for the use of natural resources and areas to the various administrative and political institutions and levels.

In many ways the act was a signal of changing attitudes and policies in a regime heavily dependent on economic expertise and macro-oriented planning. The new law was a move from a predominant economic planning policy to a planning system where also architects and social scientists were enrolled as experts by the administration. It was also a signal of the increased regulatory problems in a society dependent on large and complex technological systems. It may also be seen as the first of several steps to move both decisions and responsibility for the new problems from the central administration to the local communities.

3. Institution-Building, 1970 - 1980

The second phase saw the field become politicised, institutionalised and further integrated and an environmental science and technology policy sector gradually evolved. Four "events" underline these points. In 1970, demonstrators tried to stop the construction of a hydropower dam in Mardøla. Even though they were removed and the dam built, the action definitively placed the environment as a central theme on the public and political agenda. While many environmental organisations were established in the 1960s, it was first in the 1970s that they took centre stage in the public arena. The three most important organisations of this phase were *snm*, the Norwegian Nature Protection Union (NNV) and the "Future in Our Own Hands" (FIVH). In addition to the central roles they played, they also represented quite different ideologies and strategies.

Two years later, the Ministry of Environment *(MD)* was established. This event can be related to different problems; first, the difficulties in handling and co-ordinating the various administrative tasks related to the environment in a satisfactory way, and secondly, the desire on behalf of some actor-groups to set up an administrative apparatus that could challenge the superiority of the *Ministry of Finance (MF)*, thus changing the direction of social and economic development.

In 1970, the Norwegian Council for Science and Technology *(NTNF)* appointed a committee that was to initiate and finance research projects to detect, supervise and develop means to halt pollution. Even though the Norwegian Research Council for Science and Humanities (NAVF) and The Norwegian Council for Agricultural Research (NLVF) already had small programs running and NIVA, NILU and NIBR were doing research, the appointment of the Committee on Pollution (KF) was the first serious attempt to speed up the science and technology initiatives in this sector. Even if this set up was initiated by the science system itself, it must be regarded a part of the new general policy showing the diffusion of ideas between various domains.

In 1971, a comprehensive plan for the development of the Norwegian highway system, Norwegian Plan for Highways No. 1 *(NVP1)* was passed in Parliament. The plan was accepted as such, but the proposal gave rise to serious criticism. Several of the members of Parliament criticised the plan for being technocratic. They also called for "counter-expertise" to confront ministerial expertise. This incident points to the central role of scientific expertise in societal planning, it also showed the build-up of environmentally

78

related topics in research sectors other than the natural sciences. It also underlined a growing problem related to expert roles.

4. The First Wave of Environmentalism

Started in 1914, the "old" organisation the Norwegian nature protection union *(NNV)* sought from the very start to preserve natural areas containing special Norwegian features. Even if the nationalism disappeared, the preservation ideology was strong until the middle of the 1960s. At that point, *NNV* together with the Tourist Association, the Norwegian Association of Hunters and Anglers and a youth organisation called 4H, launched a new campaign. What initially had been a fight for natural parks now became a general struggle to preserve all natural areas. "Use your consciousness to preserve nature" became the organisations' new slogan. The slogan indicates the strong relation between knowledge and education and environmentalism. While *NNV* had 5 000 members in 1965, the number rose to 20 000 in 1973, with 18 local groups scattered all over the country (Berntsen 1977: 87, 126-129).

Established in 1969, *snm* was a "young" organisation. *Snm* took up questions related to the intensive investment in hydro-power plants and the problems caused by mass automobile traffic. At *Mardøla* plans were made for exploiting Europe's highest waterfall. As national and natural monument, it was the perfect place to awake the public and the politicians. *Snm* first opposed the plan with "soft" methods by publishing articles and lobbying in Parliament. When Parliament decided to go on with the project *snm* organised a camp near the waterfall. Some week later the demonstrators, chained together, were cut loose and removed by the police. Television and newspapers covered the incident in minute detail and this event became a turning point and a symbol of environmental concerns now being a political problem. Afterwards, *snm* spread to other universities and efforts were made to gather all environmental interests and reshape *snm* into an umbrella organisation. In 1974, there were 13 local branches all over Norway. Marxists gradually became a strong group in the organization and tried to transform it into a mass-movement organisation. A growing internal antagonism ended in 1976 when the cross-political strategy won out with a very small margin of victory. However the damage caused by this struggle never healed, and this was more or less the end of *snm* (Dahl 1994: 106-110).

The third and youngest organisation was the Future in Our Hands *(FIVH)*. In the early 1970s, the initiator Erik Damman had spent one year on a Pacific Ocean island, living the "simple" life. In 1972 he published a book (Damman 1972) in which he tried to persuade people to return to a simpler, but better way of living. A central element in his philosophy was the reduction of consumption. The public debate and interest aroused by the book led to the establishment of an organisation with the same name in 1974.

Even if *snm*, *NNV* and *FIVH* promoted many of the same ideas, it is possible to make some more general distinction related to modes of participation and their view of science and technology. All three proclaimed the need for structural changes. But while *NNV* and *snm* claimed that these changes had to be invoked through political decisions, *FIVH* believed that the changes had to be an outcome of individual efforts. Their views on participation were also different. *NNV*'s strategy was responsibility and participation, thus influencing policy-makers directly. *FIVH* and *snm* on the other hand, stood up as a counter-force to the authorities. The result of these different strategies was, in essence, that *NNV* became both a participator and an hostage, gaining limited, but somewhat noticeable influence. The counter-establishment strategy of *FIVH* and *snm* made them visible in the public debate and somewhat effective in agenda setting. Both strategies came, in different ways, to initiate protests and action, and thus opening the stage for changes.

Both *snm* and *NNV* stated the need for "a better knowledge" of nature. This "knowledge" points towards *snm* and *NNV*'s close connection to academia and to science. When it comes to *FIVH*, the picture is more blurry. Their view and focus was more "lay knowledge" and "common sense" oriented than expertise oriented. When it came to technology, both *NNV* and *snm* addressed technology in their writings. *NNV*, in the same way as *snm*, promoted the view that new and better technology would benefit the environment. But whereas *snm* argued for ecologically sound solutions (what they called soft technologies), *NNV*'s argued for better technology (what we may call end-of-pipe technologies). *FIVH* was simply not interested in these questions.

A last point that connects both lines was that while *NNV* was an organisation that wanted "growth with protection", *snm* and *FIVH* promoted a "limits to growth" perspective. In the same way as earlier, this linked *NNV* to the administration and existing policy, while *snm* and *FIVH* were more related to the *international* ecological debate.

When the Ministry of the Environment (*MD*) was established in 1972 it was a result of several factors, including the preservationist ideas as articulated by *NNV*, the need to secure areas for recreation (brought forward by both idealist industrialists and the labour movement), the early ecological views as presented by *snm*, the international achievements in this sector and the need for a more rational administration with regard to resource questions. On the other side the establishment of the Ministry reflected the administration's own need to deal with the tensions caused by the modernisation process and come up with science and technology measures.

In 1971 the Commission on Resources finished its work with a divided proposal for a ministry of the environment. While the majority of the commission wanted a powerful "over-department" that could overrule the other sectorial ministries, the minority proposed a ministry which would coordinate all public efforts to regulate, supervise and secure the environment (Ustvedt 1981: 449-450). At the same time there was a change of government. A block of liberal parties which had held the power from 1969 to 1971 was replaced by the Labour Party. Since the new Labour government disagreed with the majority block proposal they set up a new commission, the Himle-Commission. This commission moved the discussion from the political to the ministerial arena and thus closed off the debate. Not unexpectedly it came up with a proposal for a co-ordinating, not a decision making ministry. This conflict between different policies is important and has remained as one of the main controversies up to the present. During the 1970s the various science and technology initiatives came to mill about in this administrative no-man's land.

The new ministry came to be dominated by civil servants from other departments, especially from the Ministry of Municipalities *(KD)*. As an example, the planning division was to a large extent created by moving the division for the development of the rural areas to *MD*. In many ways this also illustrates an attempt on behalf of the established technical-economical and technocratic planning tradition of the 1960s to be reshaped for "modern times".

The intensive use of civil servants and legal practitioners from the established ministries caused criticism. University scientists signed a petition, where they pointed out three main problems. The first was the extensive use of economists and lawyers, what was called persons without biological and social science knowledge. Secondly, the narrow scope of these persons' views on environmental matters was questioned. Thirdly, the need for technical expertise to evaluate and to communicate with industry was raised (Jansen 1989: 225-227). In addition to criticism from "'external' actor groups", *MD* from the very start was engaged in disputes with the other more centrally placed ministries such as Ministry of Industry (MI) and the Treasury. Criticism was not directed against the division for nature and the outdoor life because it tried to establish links to environmental organisations. The various types of criticism indicate the most obvious problems of *MD* in this phase: to integrate environmental considerations into the overall policy making process, the lack of credibility in relation to other actors in the same domain, and the lack of expertise to establish science and technology policy measures.

In 1970, *NTNF* appointed the Committee of Pollution (*FK*) to fund and guide environmental research projects. In the years from 1970 to 1985 *FK* funded several projects. One major project was set up to examine the causes and consequences of acid rain on the forest and inland fish resources, another was to create a distant monitoring system of sea and air pollution, a third project was to improve methods for detecting and removing chemical and biological pollution. Several other projects dealt with the basic problems related to the management of solid and liquid waste, the development of better technical equipment to deal with air and water pollution. These solutions were much in the spirit of the time, that is to say, end-of-pipe technologies.

The Acid Rain Project was carried out in the years between 1972 and 1980. The reason for the program was a suspicion that acid rain was the cause of damage to the forest and the increasing death of fish in the southern parts of Norway. Since forestry was an economically more important trade than inland fishery, the focus first came on acid rain's impact on forests. While the project was initiated by *FK*, from 1973 the Ministry of the Environment *(MD)* was deeply involved in the project. When *MD* joined in, the focus on forest damages and air pollution came to overshadow all other types of acidification. Since *MD* participated in international programs on long range transport of pollution, it needed quick responses. The ministry used its administrative muscle to delimit the focus and speed up the work for "findings". This was opposed by academic researchers who questioned the narrow scope of the project. Research should be carried out according to scientific standards and not with fast and simple results as the major aim, they claimed. *MD* on the other side, criticised the independent academic researchers for destroying an important international initiative to stop long range pollution.

This short description shows the tension between academic scientists' struggle for independence and the administrative need of quick responses. It also stresses the problematic connection between the administration's goal oriented ideals and academia's scientific and independence ideals. These limited conflicts direct our attention towards another line in science and technology policy formation, the counter-expertise strategy.

In the late 1950s and early 1960s Norwegian society experienced dramatic growth in the number of cars. In addition to the real growth, engineers and economists promoted a strong belief in the coming of the thoroughly motorised society. The factual situation and the proclaimed visions moved the techno-economic expertise into positions where they could influence the planning of the future transport system in an substantial way. Large state initiated planning projects became new strongholds for technocratic expertise.

The Norwegian Plan for Highways no. 1 (NVP1) was carried out in the years between 1964 and 1969. The mandate given the planning committee, consisting of three economists and three engineers, was to lay out a scheme for the investments in the main Norwegian roads for the period 1970 to 1990. The finished plan, published in 1969, was built mainly on technical and economic considerations. The smooth flow of traffic with as little use as possible of resources bringing cars from one point to another was the main ideal of the committee (Østby 1995).

When the plan was made public, it was met by heavy criticism. The criticism can be divided into two main groups. The first was a demand from all parts of Norway for more resources for the roads in their own district. The second was disapproval from various groups, arguing that the plan was centralised, sectorial, technocratic and narrowly based on technical and economical variables.

While the first criticism underlines the dominant values for social development of that time, the latter was a sign of new groups entering the arena of research. In Parliament the same arguments were stated and some of the constituents called for counter-expertise to meet ministerial expertise. This illustrates another situation where the general public, through its representatives tried to influence the direction of science and technology policy development. While *NVP1* was being concluded, a new plan Norwegian Plan for Highways 2 (*NVP2*), was initiated. This time planning should be carried out as a decentralised process where nearly 80 local committees should be heard. Not only engineers and economists, but also architects and social scientists were engaged in the planning activities. A final but important point was that the mandate explicitly stated that environmental questions should be considered in a serious way. At this stage, not only representatives, but also lay people were called to participate in hearings.

Since the resources available for establishing separate and independent research institutes were limited, environmental organisations had to find alternative ways to integrate their views and expertise. One was to make their own alternative reports to counter the administrative reports. Another was the work carried out by researchers inside traditional research institutions and the universities. Some institutions became from the very start sites for alternative and radical views on social planning and development. The third type of counter-expertise strategy was to get access to state planning projects. During the 1970s, radical, anti-establishment and anti-positivist researchers came to work in institution serving state policy. This led to a change in scope and direction for many research projects.

Even if the impact of these counter-expertise attempts is difficult to measure, there is some indirect evidence. Even if the counter-expertise could not be identified as deriving from separate institutions, the impact of independent radical researchers and institutions was seen as a problem by the administration. In order to contain what was termed "interest-dominated" research, "The Langslet-doctrine" was launched in 1981 by the Conservative government. According to this doctrine, funding of research should in principle, or to a greater extent, be directed by "neutral" research councils and not by ministries. The Langslet doctrine was first of all a continuation of the belief in neutral science and positivism. Secondly, it was an attempt to regulate the relation between administration and science, and thus counter the impact of counter-expertise, the radicalisation of professionals and the incorporation of radical views in research.(cf. Eide 1995: 50-51)

Another central theme of the 1970s was the energy question. In the 1950s Norway was among the first countries to construct nuclear reactors. But the attempts to make this a new source of energy did not succeed. The use of water resources seemed more promising than this new technology. In the 1970s, the question was raised anew, but this time the proposal was put aside after heavy protests from the general public, environmental organisations and not the least by the incidents in Harrisburg, Pennsylvania (Berntsen 1994: 203ff).

Concerning the construction of hydro-power plants, the development continued in more or less the same tracks as it had started in the beginning of the century. Several plans were made to protect the remaining waterfalls, but the protection of nature was mainly done in areas that were of little or no public interest. Two white papers, *The resource situation for Norway in a global perspective* and *Natural resources and economic development* published in the mid-1970s clearly defined the governmental perspectives with a further building up of energy intensive industry as still the main goal. The reports showed the marginal gains of environmental organisations related to the energy-industry alliance.

The policy strategy of these papers made the environmental organisations come up with their own reports. The physicist Hugo Parr chaired a committee that created a counter-report with a clear request that the heavy exploitation of energy sources had to be stopped. *Energy, environment and society* was clearly inspired by international ideas of "limits to growth". But as a means to change the established trajectory, this publication seemed to be produced in vain. As a policy-making instrument it seemed, at best, to convince only its own supporters.

Consequently, the 1970s culminated the same way as they started, with a conflict related to the construction of a hydropower dam, this time in Alta, Finnmark in 1980. From the time that the project was presented in 1971, until the major conflict in 1980, there was continued protests against its construction from various action-groups. From 1978, the People's Initiative to stop the Alta-construction (*FMA*) came to co-ordinate and direct different actions against the construction plans. A central theme all through the battle was the prognosis about the "real" need for energy. The first prognosis made by the hydro-electrical companies themselves showed convincing figures for the future need of more energy in the region. Another prognosis made by the Bureau of Statistics reduced the figures substantially. When the prognosis was criticised, the Ministry of Industry met this challenge by pointing at the low use of energy at the moment and the great need in the future. Several other reports showed marginal economic gains. When the Alta construction was discussed in Parliament, the discrepancy between the different prognoses was pointed out. But it was all too obvious that the project had to be carried out, not the least to save the political prestige of the political elite, with Gro Harlem Brundtland as the main figure. While *MI* worked hard to support the project, *MD* played a very defensive role throughout the controversy. This role may be regarded a conclusion of *MD*'s problems in getting a stronger grip on the development of the overall policy and to create its own policies. As in 1970, at Mardøla, demonstrators were removed by a massive police force. The energy ideology of the political elite and not the least their prestige over-ruled science, local and national protest. The controversy put new focus on the relation between public engagement, the momentum of the existing official energy policy and the power of the state.

5. Reconstitution, 1982-1996

In the period from the early 1980s to the present, the modern industrial state, heavily committed to large technological system and a booming oil industry, saw the commitment to environmental protection being both integrated, professionalised and dissolved. Integrated in the respect that nearly every sector adopted the ideas of sustainability, professionalised in the way that highly trained experts became the key actors in defining and proposal making phases, and dissolved in the respect that the responsibility for environmental dangers was no longer placed only upon the central administration. The label reconstitution points at this reformulation of both definitions and policies.

An important feature of the 1980s was a structural transformation of environmentalism. Even if the lost cause of Alta had destroyed the beliefs of many activists, new organisations entered the arena. While the majority of the "old" and now more "responsible" activists joined political parties, public administration, research or sunk deeper into their sofas, new types of organisations came into being. One type was almost militant and carried out actions against industrial installations. Another new form was the establishment of local branches of international organisations in Norway. A third type were organisations that emulated consultant firms. While Nature and Youth (NU) and Bellona were the best examples of the first type, Green-peace and World Wildlife Fund (WWF) were the most influential of the second type. What we may label Bellona, version 2, represents the third type.

Closely linked to these changes was the set up and transformation of a more permanent counter-expertise experiment. After extensive lobbying by environmental organisations, Parliament in 1982 granted Alternative Future (*AF*) money for research. This counter-expertise experiment later turned into a more or less established research "institute", Research for a Sustainable Society (ProSus) exemplifying a through professional approach.

During this phase, various events put industry in the public and political focus as the major contributor to pollution. This was one reason for industry, in a very slow fashion, coming up with preventive measures. The late development of clean industry in a Norwegian context, was stated in a white paper from 1987. It concluded that Norwegian industry, contrary to its international counterparts, had been very slow to take environmental precautions. In spite of industrial aloofness, this phase saw a new weight put on environmental research and development as a major area for the future. When it happened, it was based on two arguments; first, the need integrate sustainability into this sector, and second, to find new fields of expansion for industry. This new interest had an additional side, the stress on integrating technical and social research. Environmental science and technology research should now be multidisciplinary and the need for co-ordinating research activities was especially underlined. This illustrates a shift from "end-of-pipe" to "end-of-society" solutions, pointing consequently at the later attempts to initiate cleaner technologies in the 1990s.

Since 1983 Nature and Youth (NU), the youth organisation of NNV tried to stop the emission of eliminate waste from the company Titania in Jøssing-fjorden. Eliminate, an important raw material for producers of paint, was extracted from solid rock and had to be enriched before it could be shipped to companies in Germany. The enrichment process resulted in a lot of waste that was dumped in the fjord. Many years of production had filled up the fjord and now the company planned to send the waste in pipes to the outlet of the fjord. Local fishermen had tried to stop the dumping of waste, but in vain. In 1983 environmentalists went to the outlet of the fjord to stop the construction of waste pipes. During this campaign, the activist received help from the Danish branch of Greenpeace, illustrating the emerging global scope of environmentalism. The construction was not stopped, but continued under continuous disturbance from the activists, and was covered by media.

During this new national drama several actors were brought onto the stage. One was the National Office for Pollution (SFT) directed by MD, another was The Institute for Fishing Research (IFR) and the third was a private consultancy firm, Miljøforsk. The first was a supervising agency, the second a publicly financed research institute and the third a private consultancy firm. Before SFT moved into the arena, Titania had used the results arrived at by Miljøforsk showing that only small amounts of the waste would disperse outside the dumping site. An investigation carried out by SFT and IFR later stated that this figures were far too low. The dispute ended when the authorities forced Titania to store the waste on land.

This event and the entry of new official and private research and regulatory bodies and consultancy firms onto the stage underlines the coming of new constellations in the environmental field. Private firms ordered examinations, official regulatory bodies increased their interventions and official research institutions were hired to give the "correct" answers to problems. The outcome of this conflict also points at a general change of policy, where industrial pollution is addressed in a more serious way by the state administration.

The intervention of various types of expertise in this limited controversy had an additional outcome, the creation of a new strategy for environmental organisations. In 1986, during the end of the Titania conflict, two active members of NU, Frederic Hauge and Rune Haaland, left NU and started Bellona. The initiators wanted a more professional and effective organisation than NNV and NU. Bellona was from the very start directed by its leaders with no pretensions of being democratic. In the beginning, Bellona followed the strategy of NU and carried out several actions against industrial plants. But in addition to these activities, it was heavily committed to scientific and technical expertise. Bellona also set new standards for NGOs by using the media in quite a professional way. In 1987 they started a crusade against one of the largest Norwegian corporations Norsk Hydro. Their "investigations" exposed the spill of large quantities of mercury to water and the air. Another large corporation, Borregaard was approached in the same way. By extensive use of the media, by gathering their own "scientific" samples to document the pollution, these industrial corporations, the Government and SFT were forced to take measures.

In the years after its establishment, from 1986 to 1990, Bellona was financed by its members. In 1990, after serious economic trouble, the organisation was reorganised. The new partner became industry, gradually paying nearly 75 percent of their expenses. The change of financial support was also followed by an alteration of images and methods. Instead of presenting themselves as rebels, their new style was to look like experts and consultants. They not only changed from fishermen's sweaters to Italian suits, they adopted the same ideology and language as their sponsors and were gradually regarded as serious "partners" for discussion. They moved into the same areas as the ministries' economic and technical experts. During the controversy related to EU-membership in 1994, Bellona was the only NGO arguing for a member-ship. They stood on the same side as industry and the government (Søgård 1995).

The more "traditional" organisations such as *NNV* and *FIVH* chose another route and launched an intensive lobbying campaign to convince the authorities for the need of an alternative research project (Malknes 1995). They were successful and Alternative Future (AF) was established to develop one or several knowledge-based models for alternative societies, where social, environmental and resource responsibility should be given priority over material and economic ends. Secondly, the project should examine the possibility of changing the direction of the Nordic societies towards an alternative society. Thirdly, AF should try out some of these models in small-scale practical experiments.

After few years existence the scientific establishment voiced their suspicion concerning the professional competence of this project. A Nordic evaluation group appointed to review AF ended up recommending incorporating the project into The Council for Research on Social Planning (RFSP). The initiators of AF protested and were heard. This controversy between the initiating organisations and the national research system is interesting. Behind the research system's objections one can imagine the administration's objection. Runar I. Malkenes argues that the administration made it a principle to counteract the project.

In spite of the initiators wish to keep AF independent and "counter", AF was gradually integrated into the established research system, changing its position from an independent alternative research project, to a research "institute". From 1987 AF participated in the World Commission's work in Norway, and later in the UN-meeting in Rio de Janeiro. AF launched several research projects related to the challenges discussed at the Rio conference. The project "Sustainable Economy" was an effort to set up an alternative formulation for economic development. In 1995, AF was institutionalised as the Program for research and evaluation for a sustainable society (ProSus).

On the background of their international achievements, the Brundtland government had to follow its own message in some way or another. Even if the commitments at first glance seemed to be more rhetorical than practical, administrative measures were taken. One example was Environmental Protection in the Municipalities (MIK), an attempt to create obligatory environmental offices with professional competence in the municipal administrations. Another was the Environmental Home Guard (EHG), an attempt to integrate sustainability on the grassroots level. A third was the establishment of two centres for research and education for development and environmental tasks. The Centre for Development and the Environment (SUM) was set up at the University of Oslo, and the Centre for Environment and Development (SMU) was organised at the University of Trondheim. Interestingly enough, the majority of the initiatives seem to be driven from above, with MD and the central offices of the environmental organisations, the amalgamated environmental family, as the driving forces.

An effort to integrate both "knowing and doing" on the local level was The Environmental Home Guard (MHV), established in 1990. The initiative was taken by NNV and the National Campaign for Environment and Development (FMU), and was financially supported by MD. The major goals of MHV were to reduce and change consumption patterns. Another main aim was to provide people with information about how to make more environmentally proper choices in everyday situations. A third measure was to provide the members with tools to become involved in local activities for environmental protection by creating networks of interested persons. This also included the learning of how to make their members influential in different types of ad-hoc movements, organisations, firms or local communities. A central concept for MHV was voluntary communal work which points at the traditional way to carry out local duties or activities. The name, Home Guard, also points at the old tradition of safeguarding society from the attack of enemies. Even if the Home Guard is an individualistic organisation, with individuals, families and small local groups as members, the central organisation points towards the need to combine individual actions with more structural changes (Endal 1994: 35-37).

According to the main philosophy of *MHV*, emphasis is placed on simple but concrete tasks. These tasks vary from the use of cloth baby diapers instead of paper diapers, car-pooling, separation of waste in the household, to the use of toxic chemicals in public work. One example illustrating this attempt is the municipality of Malvik near Trondheim which was picked as a test municipality. The goal of the project is to establish twenty green families in the municipalities. To get the project going the chief officer, the chief environmentalist and the personnel manager of the municipality had volunteered.

From the late 1980s, there was a gradual building up of decentralised environmental administrations. From 1987, *MIK* was set up in many local administrations. In addition to *MIK*, what was called "environmental packages", e.g. fresh money, were contributed to projects in the municipalities. The selected municipality had to prove its ability to co-ordinate different sectors and institutions, and thus invoke changes based on specific targets. These initiatives can obviously be linked to the ideas of the Brundtland Commission report and later Agenda 21. In addition it must be related to two vital Norwegian trends in the 1990s. The first is a general decentralisation of political regulation and steering. The second is the increased difficulties on behalf of the central authorities in imposing their power at the local level. The global-local timing, and the distribution of risks and control underlines the late modern aspects of these changes.

MIK was tried out in 91 municipalities and each municipality had to engage a "chief adviser for the environment". His main tasks was to initiate, co-ordinate and supervise environmental activities in different administrative sectors in each municipality. How this should be done, and which tasks had the highest priority was left to the municipalities to decide (Naustdalslid and Hovik, eds 1994). In 1990, *MIK* was evaluated by various research institutions resulting in ambiguous conclusions. Among the investigating institutions there was a general agreement that *MIK* had caused a change of interest and attitude concerning environmental policy making. However, these changes had not been substantial and were more on the discursive than the practical level. Some of the changes were due to the kind of knowledge possessed by the chief environmentalist. Even more interesting was the discovery that public opinion seemed to have little influence on the decision makers in the municipalities. The last point was the lack of contact between the local administration and local industry. Both *MIK* and *MHV* point at the obvious lack of expertise and influence, the gap between policies and practise, and the distance between central decisions and local ability to create and carry out both new policies and concrete measures.

In 1979, the Royal Norwegian Council for Scientific and Industrial Research (NTNF) conducted a more comprehensive analysis of the "the field". Attention was drawn to the lack of cooperation between various domains. In addition, the analysis stressed that while the first generation efforts had been to clean up pollution, the second should be focused on preventing further pollution. A white paper also stated the obvious need to include other types of scientific expertise such as sociology, psychology and medicine into research and development.

In 1987 NTNF started the programme Industrial Sustainable Technology, as response to the Brundtland report. The stated aim was to combine environmental precautions with industrial development and growth. The starting of this programme was followed by attempts to identify areas in which industrialisation utilizing clean industry could take place. Three areas were picked as the most interesting in the initial phase: the development of methods and equipment for long distance environmental supervision and detection, clean technology for sea-based industries and the more general development of clean industry and trade. In 1991, 11 new programmes were started. The combination of pollution prevention with export possibilities was clearly illustrated by the projects. The project FORFOR was aimed at large scale industrial production processes, EKSPOMIL had as its main goal increasing the value of exported clean production equipment and KOMTEK should improve the effectiveness and environmental aspects of municipal activities.

In 1990, Parliament passed a new chapter in the Planning and Building Act, which required industry to make environmental impact assessments (EIA). With this, industry, i.e. large and middle-sized firms, were forced to present responsible solutions and mitigating measures due to industrial changes to the state administration and other interested parties. As before, however, the administration had the authority to decide the fate of new industrial efforts. At the moment EIA seems to have become one of the most powerful means of regulation related to the environment and industry.

In 1991, a Parliamentary report concerning the environmental activities in the municipalities was put forward. After some delay the new attempt became an effort to copy the EU's directive on voluntary steering of environmental measures. This is tried by using several documents for examination, planning and revision of the environmental activities in the municipalities. The last attempt is to carry out environmental audits. By establishing rules for audits, each municipality has to secure that their "deficits" are being corrected. Both in connection with *NTNF* and these administrative regulations we can clearly see the move from so called end-of-pipe technologies to "upstream anticipation", a mixture of process, product and product-chain oriented measures. The principle of prevention instead of reaction, has lead to closer focus on the early stages of product life cycles (Aall 1995: 62-65).

6. Concluding Remarks

This article has attempted to map out a comprehensive field. I have tried to point out central actor-groups and important incidents. I have tried to show a gradual change in the environmental field through three overlapping, but different phases. With regard to the phase-model the changes seem to be as follows:

The late 1950s and the 1960s were a time of "problem identification". In this phase, the problem was a many-sided and flexible concern related to the tensions caused by the modern industrial state. The untouched natural areas and the traditional ways of living were to be protected. The solutions proposed were better regulations, new laws and increased scientific knowledge. Different initiatives such as the establishment of research institutions, royal commissions and the passing of new acts were tried out. In this situation, science gradually came to be the main base for further negotiations of both problems and policies. In spite of more precise formulations of problems and policies, it remained a fragmented field.

The second phase, from 1970 up to the early 1980s was a breakthrough for environmental groups and thus for "environmentalism". In the same period, administrative measures were set up to address environmental problems in a more over-arching way. The main problem was determined to be the destruction of the inner cities by the increased use of private cars and the destruction of nature by the intensive exploitation of the water resources. The remedies were administrative and technical: integration of environmental considerations, regulations and solutions into all sectors of the society, and the creation of end-of-pipe remedies to clean the worst types of pollution to air and water.

The third phase, between the years 1983 and 1996, was in many ways a time of reorganisation of both civil society and administrative initiatives. A new type of more specialised NGO entered the arena, and the focus turned from energy and transport towards big industry. The end-of-pipe policy was reformulated towards cleaner production and, in a more limited fashion, technology assessment. Another feature of this period was the professionalisation and technocratisation of the field. The greening of all sectors of society has made expertise an obligatory point of passage for further negotiations between the various domains. In that respect public participation on the policy level has been dependent on highly skilled and trained experts.

References

Aall, Carlo (1995) "Bordet fanger" i *Alternativ framtid nr. 3 1995*: 62 - 65

Berntsen, Bredo (1994) *Grønne linjer - Natur og Miljøvernets historie i Norge*. Oslo: Grøndahl Dreyer.

Brox, Ottar (1966) *Hva skjer i Nord-Norge*. Oslo: Pax

Dahl, Thomas (1994) *Ordering Nature - Environmentalism as a Cultural Phenomenon*, Doctoral Thesis at Roskilde University Centre, Denmark

Damman, Erik (1972) *Fremtiden i våre hender: Om hva vi alle kan gjøre for å styre utviklingen mot en bedre verden* (Foreword by Arne Næss), Oslo: Gyldendal

Eide, Kjell (1995) *Vitenskapeliggjøring av politikk*. Oslo: Utrednings-instituttet

Endal, Dag (1994) "Citizen Mobilization for Environmental Protection and Sustainable Consumption" in William M Lafferty (ed.): *Steps Towards Sustainable Consumption*, Oslo: Rerport from Prosjekt Alternativ Framtid

Malknes, Runar (1995) "En alternativ fortid" i *Tidsskriftet alternativ framtid* nr 4

Naustdalslid, Jon and Hovik, Sissel, eds (1994) Lokalt miljøvern. Otta: Norwegian Institute for Urban and Regional Research

Næss, Arne (1972) *Økologi og filosofi*, Oslo: Universitetsforlaget, 1972

Næss, Arne (1976) *Økologi, samfunn og livsstil*, Oslo: Universitetsforlaget

Roll-Hansen, Nils and Hestmark, Geir (1990) *Miljøforskning mellom viten-skap og politikk, Utredninger om forskning og høyere utdanning*, NAVFs utredningsinstitutt, Norges Allmennvitenskapelige forskningsråd

Søgård, Christin (1995) *Fra rebeller til konsulenter. En sociologisk studie av miljøstiftelsen Bellona.* Masters thesis in sociology, University of Bergen

Ustvedt, Yngvar (1981): *Overflod og oppgjør - Det skjedde i Norge Bind 3 1961 - 72*, Oslo: Gyldendal

Lithuania: Environmental Awareness and National Independence

by Leonardas Rinkevicius[1]

1. Introduction

In the case of Lithuania, the public engagement in environmental science and technology policy is closely interrelated with the overall transformation and democratization of Lithuanian society since the late 1980s. Particularly important are two parallel but integrated processes, namely the emergence and growth of public environmental awareness, and the awakening and maturation of a national consciousness and identity that led to the re-establishment of the national state of Lithuania.

The Green movement of Lithuania played probably the most important role as a catalyst of public participation, particularly at the early stage of societal transformation. It gave rise to public environmental awareness, translated environmental concern into actions that affected environmental and technological decisions on the state level. Differently from the environmental movements in Western countries in the 1970s, the green movements in Eastern Europe attracted not only people from delimited

[1] I would like to thank my colleague, Dalia Gineitiene, for her research contribution in reviewing historical development of the green movement in Lithuania. This work has resulted into a Master's thesis by Dalia Gineitiene "The Role of the Lithuanian Green Movement in Decision Making". This research as well as Dalia's comments on earlier draft of this paper were very informative and valuable.

parts of society, like students or nature-lovers, but rather they mobilized society at large, because environmental critique was a crucial part of the critique of the totalitarian state regime.

The greens were very active in making public space for communicating new ideas and world views and transferring them to other parts of society. The greens can therefore be characterized as one of the cornerstones that paved the way to the cultural revival and re-establishment of the national state of Lithuania. Therefore, the review of experiences of public participation in environmental science and technology policy in Lithuania will to a large extent be a review of the development of the Lithuanian Green movement.

On the other hand, the intersection or even integration of environmental science and technology policy discourse with the discourse on the restoration of the state of Lithuania has in common not only cultural and social dimensions, but also particular controversial technical-economic issues. The nuclear power plant at Ignalina as well as the case of construction of an oil terminal on the coast of the Baltic Sea are examples of such issues. They were and still are of major public importance, and subject to widespread concern and disagreement. We will discuss these cases later in this paper.

2. Environmentalism in Lithuania: Historical Background

The history of environmentalism in Lithuania can be traced in the Salynas' agreement, the document of the 14th century when the first attempt was made to protect "saintly woods" which were important for both religious, defensive and economic reasons. The ban on felling old oaks which were considered saintly trees in pagan Lithuania was passed as early as 1420. In the later legal documents of the 15th and 16th centuries, particularly in the

Statutes of Lithuania[2] and land reform documents, forestry, hunting, beekeeping, and fishing were discussed and penalties for violations were proposed (Januskis 1990; Gineitiene 1996). In particular, the seasons for hunting and fishing were defined in order not to destroy natural reproduction of various species by human intervention. In the following centuries, when Lithuania was incorporated into Poland and later was occupied by czarist Russia, some of these laws were suspended or ceased to function. The close feeling of harmony with nature, however, remained characteristic of the culture of Lithuanian peasants. It is reflected in folk songs, tales, habits and traditions.

> According to the moral culture of village people, humans exist in nature and must live in harmony with its forces and phenomena.... A specific features differentiating humans from other phenomena of nature is their ability to work. However, the human labor can be regarded as a homogenous particle of nature only if it is *performed in nature* [my italics - L.R.], when man works together with nature, thereby paying honor to it. (Kavolis 1994:130)

Even discussing the issue of alienation of Jewish people in Lithuanian communities, some authors suggest that the reason for this is not, the traditional belief in their responsibility for the crucifixion of Jesus Christ and related controversial issues in the history of Christianity, but rather it is the traditional occupation of the Jews as merchants, craftsmen, traders.

---

[2] The statutes of the Grand Duchy of Lithuania of 1528, 1566 and 1588 are regarded as most progressive and liberal state legal documents in Europe of that time, especially in terms of care about humans, their beliefs and freedom of religion, cosmology, values, including environmental ones (cf Kavolis, 1994).

These kinds of jobs were not in accordance with "work in nature" and thus not respectable by the standrads of Lithuanian peasants (cf Kavolis 1994).

In the 20th century, particularly during the short period of re-established independence between the two world wars, peasants and farmers made up the largest proportion of the Lithuanian population (about 80% in 1923, and 77 % in 1939). This period was significant as a time of revival and there was a mix of pagan and Christian values and an emphasis on the traditional peasant communities. It would not be an exaggeration to say that in the first half of the 20th century many Lithuanians were still representing the so-called Arcadian tradition (cf Worster 1977) where man was seen as a part of nature, living in close harmony with it.

> A saintly feeling of respect to nature was characteristic in the traditional Lithuanian culture. There was no need for individuals having a pagan way of thinking to explain ecological problems as at every turn of their lives they felt dependence upon nature and behaved accordingly. (Kalenda, 1992:16).

In this inter-war period, there took place a parallel development of public initiatives as well as public policies in the field of nature protection. The Government of Lithuania passed several laws and regulations such as the Law on Hunting, Rules on Fishing, the Law on Forestry, the Law on Nature Research Station and others (Marcijonas, 1978).

Similarly to the Western countries, the public in Lithuania was actively participating in nature protection activities, especially nature conservation. In 1921, the Association to Adorn Lithuania was established on the initiative of the famous priest and writer J. Tumas-Vaizgantas. The Association to Adorn Lithuania saw its task as reviving the war-torn nature, as well as in raising public interest in spiritual values. (Valionyte, 1996). Similarly, the so-called Committee for Planting Trees was set up in 1923, and the Lithuanian Society of Naturalists (*Lietuvos Gamtininku draugija*) was established in 1931. These were important steps towards increased public environmental awareness aimed at harmonizing relations between humans and nature.

After the Second World War the situation in Lithuania changed dramatically. With coming of the Soviet rule, most of the nature protection initiatives and organizations were terminated. One of the significant dimensions of Soviet ideology was a claim that nature must serve human needs, and that man is the master of nature. This trend recalls what Worster (1977) characterized as the imperial tradition in environmental world views. However, even the Soviet ideology could not completely eliminate environmental awareness.

Lithuania was the first republic in the USSR to establish a State Nature Protection Committee in 1957. The Committee concentrated on protection of important unique nature areas, plants and animals. In the course of development of other institutions and ministries, there emerged administrative bodies which regulated environmental activities in industrial, agricultural, energy, transportation enterprises. A Nature Protection Society was established in 1960, which, however, was "public" only to a limited extent, because the Soviet regime allowed public organizations to function within strictly defined ideological boundaries.

A national park in Aukstaitija, three nature reserves as well as 174 landscape and 74 hunting reserves were established in Lithuania during the Soviet period. The state protection covered 194 parks, 546 old trees, 116 geological sites, 250 species of rare plants, all songbirds. (Lithuania, 1986). Lithuania was also the first among the Republics of the Soviet Union to pass the Law on Nature Protection in 1959. Other regulations concerning nature protection such as Codes of Land Protection (1970), Code of Water Protection (1972), Code of Forest Protection (1977) were adopted as well (Januskis, 1990).

These and other developments were to a large extent an achievement not of the Soviet policy structures, but rather of strong individuals such as the legendary chairman of the State Nature Protection Committee. These people were able to raise environmental awareness, convince key persons in the Soviet bureaucracy, and mobilize people even in the years of oppression by the command regime (Lietuvos rytas 1996.01.20)[3]. Most people who belonged to the Soviet bureaucracy in Lithuania (top leaders of the communist party, the government, municipal administration) were born before the Second World war. Their education and socialization often took place in the pre-war "Gemeinschaft" type communities which formed a nucleus of Lithuanian society, and which rested on peasant values.

Of course, it was difficult and even dangerous to resist the drastic expansion of the Soviet industry that developed with a neglect of environmental issues. However, even without explicit public pressure there were environmental inspectors who took the risk to suspend construction of particular plants that were very important for the Soviet economy. For example, there was temporarily suspended construction of

---

[3] An example of establishment of the National park in Aukstaitija in 1968 can be taken to illustrate the type of issues which such environmental innovators and civil servants had to deal with. The main "problem" to get all permits needed for establishment of this park was the word "national" in its official legal name. It was suggested to exclude this word by the leaders of the communist party. Only long explanations by Mr. Bergas that this is the way such parks are called all over the world allowed to keep this word and establish the park (Lietuvos rytas, 1996.01.20).

the oil refinery in Mazeikiai and electronics plant Nuklonas in Siauliai[4]. The way environmental authorities have developed in Lithuania in the Soviet times and the way they affected particular industrial and technological projects indicates that there was a certain common pro-environmental perspective shared by a number of people, decision-makers as well as common citizens.

The environmental concern of that time is reflected not only in the facts of establishment of state environmental authorities, issuing laws, or temporarily suspending construction of particular industrial sites. While the Soviet system often imposed dramatic limitations to what people could do as citizens, consumers or employees, they could still shape environmental science and technology policy options in different ways.

First of all it applies to various environmentally-informed novelties and changes (rationalizations) in industry. The concept of "low- and non-waste technology" that originated in the USSR (since about the mid-1970s)[5] was well-known and developed to a certain extent in Lithuania.

---

[4]. Personal conversation with Mr. Czechavicius (21 March, 1996) who is one of the few people in Lithuania which used to work in various environmental regulatory agencies in the Soviet times, and was one of those brave environmental administrators. He still works in local environmental authorities today.

[5] Some relevant references on non- and low-waste technology (in Russian) are:

* Laskorin B.N. (1976). *Forecast of the development of technological processes and schemes*, in the proceedings of the First Symposium on 'Theoretical and Technical-economic Issues of Low- and Non-Waste Technology'. Dresden, GDR. Published by NIITEchim, Moscow.

* All Union's scientific-technical conference on 'Scientific-technical basis for creation of non-waste production'. Czernogolovka, 1977.

* Kafarov V.V. (1982). *The Principles of Non-waste Chemical Production*. Moscow, Chimya publishers.

Such an approach has been invented in the Western world under the label of pollution prevention on the single company basis (3M in 1975), and under the label of "industrial ecology" or "industrial metabolism" on the municipal or regional level.

Probably, the main difference between non-waste technology and industrial ecology is its economic dimension. The former concept, embedded in the centrally planned economy, primarily focused on the technical change, while, by contrast, the concept of industrial ecology emphasizes that "closing the loop" should be economically viable and cost-effective. In this respect, industrial ecology or industrial metabolism can be viewed as an integral part of ecological modernization (cf. Hajer 1996, Mol 1995).

In the case of Lithuania, the advancement of non-waste technology is reflected in several state documents and programs. Probably the best known is the so-called State Complex Program 82.22 aimed at the reduction and treatment of waste water and solid waste from machine tool manufacturers and electroplating companies. Part of the program was based on utilization galvanic sludge and residual oil in the ceramics factory in Palemonas (Decision of the Council of Ministers of Lithuanian SSR Nr. 211p, 1986.05.30). Initiated in 1982, this program comprised substantial R&D activities assigned to R&D institutes of the Lithuanian Academy of Sciences. A great number of industrial enterprises, state committees and ministries were enrolled in this program by the top-down order of the Council of Ministers. This program as well as other developments in low- and non-waste technology can be viewed as indicating a shift in policy-making from the nature-orientation of the 1950s and 1960s to a more technocratic approach in the 1980s.

The case of utilization of galvanic sludge and waste oil in the Palemonas ceramics factory was rather famous, and was frequently referred to in the Soviet literature on low-waste technology. The most interesting thing was not the development of technical solutions to particular problems, but the way the centrally planned system brought various actors and institutions into new public partnerships involving regulators, industries and academicians. The inventory of waste water and waste was made by companies based on inventory purchased materials[6]. Enterprises were controlled by state authorities and made publicly accountable based on this inventory as well as documented delivery of waste to Palemonas. This whole process of public policy change can be interpreted as a kind of ecological modernization in the conditions of a planned economy and a command style of regulation.

Another example of environmentally-informed public engagement in scientific and technological change were the activities of so-called "rationalizers", the people (usually engineers and workers) who through their enthusiasm and creativity contributed with a vast number of incremental innovations. These innovations often led to improved production efficiency, work safety, resource and energy saving. These innovators were rewarded financially: it was done in a centrally-planned way according to instructions issued by the State Committee of Invention and Innovation in Moscow. They were also encouraged morally; awarded with diplomas, pictures on the bulletin board of honorable workers, their contributions were publicized in factory newspapers. The number of proposed and implemented so-called rationalization options was one of the indicators according to which companies' achievements in accomplishing five-year plans were measured. In every former Soviet republic, including Lithuania, there existed a society, or association of rationalizers with local branch organizations.

---

[6] It can be compared with and seen as a predecessor of TRI - Toxics Release Inventory - system in the USA today. The latter is often mentioned as one of the most significant recent developments in the US regarding public-policy interface in the environmental field.

The third area of environmental awareness-raising and public involvement were the nature conservation (as well as historical and cultural heritage preservation) clubs and societies. In Lithuania, they often were institutionalized within tourism clubs and folk music groups (usually based at universities and research institutes). Such clubs were rather popular among students. The first Lithuanian green clubs - the core of the emerging movement - evolved out of such clubs in the late 1980s. Students expressed environmental concern through such clubs by organizing summer expeditions, collecting folk songs and tales from elder people in Lithuanian villages, organizing nature conservation work in nature reserves and parks. Students of engineering and natural sciences were also very active in summer work camps on industrial sites. The work, for example, in constructing small-scale dams on various rivers was the practical way in which a certain environmental orientation was shaped and articulated. It was a kind of socialization process, a public space for exchanging and developing ideas and opinions regarding environmentally-responsible development. Currently, intensive public discussions in Lithuania are focusing upon the the nuclear power plant at Ignalina. In this discourse, many of the voices advocating renewable energy are people whose socialization took place in the students work camps and nature expeditions.

When Gorbachev's perestroika started, the allowed boundaries of the public discussions on environmental issues were broken more and more frequently. Probably the most famous and illuminating is the case of the oil drilling in the Curonian lagoon on the Baltic Sea. A large group of well-known Lithuanian and Russian writers, artists, and academicians sent a letter to the editor of the *Literaturnaya Gazeta* in Moscow, a liberal newspaper of Perestroika times. They protested in this letter against oil extraction in the Baltic Sea on the Lithuanian coast. The letter was published in Moscow in November, 1986 which was an extremely brave step for the time.

Later it was allowed to re-print this letter in the Lithuanian newspaper *Literatura ir menas* (Literature and Art), and it was widely discussed. In the letter the uniqueness of the Curonian peninsula was described and its cultural meaning for the Lithuanian nation expressed. The arguments were also based on data from the Lithuanian Academy of Sciences. The interesting fact is that this letter was signed more by artists than by academicians, because the former had more influence on the public at that time. The protest against the project of oil extraction in the Baltic Sea received wide support from the public encompassing different groups of Lithuanian society. The plans that had developed in a Moscow research institute to drill in the Baltic and destroy an almost sacred piece of nature were terminated, although currently the authorities of Kaliningrad administered from Moscow are raising the question of oil extraction once again.

The case of oil extraction in the Curonian bay fueled public activism, and encouraged the belief that the times "they are a changing", and that intellectuals as well as common citizens can shape technological and industrial development. Intellectuals played an important role in this period of awakening. In the western world, such personalities and intellectuals as Rachel Carson and Barry Commoner expressed early warning signals of environmental concern to society based on their knowledge in the natural sciences. By contrast, the environmental awakening in Lithuania was stimulated by people who had nothing to do with science, instead they were well-known men and women in art and literature. Moreover, those people acted *in corpore*, rather than as single writers warning about negative consequences of technological and industrial expansion.

3. Public Participation in the Period of Upsurge of Perestroika

The democratization of society led to dramatic changes in 1988 and 1989. Public participation in environmental and technological debates was an important part of the crucial transformation in Lithuanian society (as in most of Central and Eastern Europe). The establishment of the first ecological clubs, namely "Atgaja" in Kaunas, "Zemyna" in Vilnius and "Zvejone" in Klaipeda in 1987 can be regarded as the beginning of the environmental movement in Lithuania. Those clubs were formed by people (mainly young) previously active members of the clubs of nature tourism, as well as organizers and participants of folk and historical expeditions. During this period, the communist party encouraged the creation of youth clubs under the guidance of the young communist league - the Komsomol. As a consequence the first green clubs were formally associated with the latter organization.

At the beginning, the greens saw their task in nature protection and conservation of the monuments of Lithuanian history. However, the green clubs and other groups gradually started raising new issues that challenged the ideological line. The examples of such issues of concern were the Ignalina nuclear power plant, the large chemical plants, and some of the military bases. The discourse ranged from technical-economic issues and environmental hazards of particular plants to a questioning of the very principles of the Soviet rule that led to such scientific and technological monsters.

In 1988, the green clubs and activists began to mobilize their forces into a common discursive space and action platform. The Green Movement emerged as a more structured, formal organization. Sajudis, Lithuania's movement for national independence and revival, was formally established at approximately the same time as the Green movement. The emergence and mobilization of the Lithuanian Greens and a simultaneous process in

Sajudis was marked by visible, large-scale actions. In July-August 1988, the first mass ecological protest actions, organized by the Greens together with Sajudis took place all over Lithuania (the Ecological Protest March, the Ecological Bicycle Tour, Rock March as well as such actions as "Save the Baltic Sea!" and "The Circle of Life"). During all the marches, actions and public rallies in various places of Lithuania ecological issues were raised, particular scientific and technological options and decisions questioned and criticized. The ideas of Sajudis about national revival and democracy were promulgated in connection to environmental critique. In 1988-1989, under the influence of these marches the Green Movement spread all across Lithuania, and many new environmental clubs and groups emerged.

In 1988, the anti-military protest was expressed primarily in environmental language without explicit political claims, whereas in 1989 the "Atgaja" club organized a Peace March throughout the country which was not only ecological but explicitly anti-military as well. This march was directed against the Soviet military bases and airports, and it was demanded that the Soviets withdraw their army from the occupied country. Ecological protest was transformed into a protest against the Soviet totalitarian system.

The Lithuanian Greens were led by people who became key figures because of their professional knowledge, ability to inspire and mobilize people and promulgate important messages. Probably the two most visible and outstanding personalities were Saulius Gricius, an engineer by education, the spiritual and organizational leader of the Atgaja club in Kaunas and the whole movement, and Zigmas Vaisvila, professional physicist and nuclear energy specialist who spent many years as a researcher at one of the institutes near Moscow that was doing military R&D.

In October 1988, the first Assembly of the Lithuanian Green Movement declared the principles of the movement, which were "to protect everything that is created by nature and to look for an alternative to the current technologies and life-style" (Gudavicius, 1988:3). In this respect, the "alternative project" of Lithuanian greens in the late 1980s reminiscent of the counterculture in the West in the late 1960s and early 1970s. The call for "alternative technologies" and "alternative life-styles" can be seen not just as a kind of environmental protest, but rather as a part of a radical liberation of Lithuanian society at large, reflecting the people' desire to break completely with the former regime, hence, with its technologies and life-styles as well.

The period of awakening and organization of the Lithuanian green movement coupled with the movement for national independence Sajudis was important not only because the environmental issues were raised, but it was the first time people realized they could express their attitudes, discuss and analyze facts openly, and most importantly, have an impact on governmental decisions.

4. The Case of Ignalina Nuclear Power Plant

The case of Ignalina Nuclear Power Plant can be presented as an important example of public influence upon decision-making of this period. In 1973, it was planned to construct in Lithuania the largest nuclear power plant in the world with 3 reactors RBMK - the same type as those in Chernobyl. All strategic plans and technical design were made in Moscow, at the Research Institute for the Exploitation of Nuclear Energy. At that time nobody considered the needs of Lithuanian society alone, all decisions were made considering the needs of the entire so-called North-Western region of the USSR. Neither scientists nor the government of Lithuania opposed this plan. It was a time of deep stagnation in the Soviet bloc when the public was silenced and could not oppose or question development plans most of which were not made public.

The first block started working in 1984, the second one in 1986, and the foundation for the third block was already laid. However, the Chernobyl catastrophe in 1986 made the public aware of the potential dangers, the people of Lithuania experienced direct consequences of this disastrous accident, although without such tragic losses as in the Ukraine and Belarus. It gave a strong impulse for re-thinking the values on which the Soviet economy was based., it also gave a strong impetus for spreading in Lithuanian society an "existential" concern. Public anxiety was deepening, while the people had little information. The opportunities were very small for public questioning of Ignalina. This kind of public anxiety can be compared with and conceptualized in terms of "risk society" (cf Beck 1992). In 1988, several articles appeared in Lithuanian newspapers where controversial facts about the potential threats of the Ignalina nuclear power plant were revealed. These articles indicated that the Ignalina plant had been constructed without an adequate environmental impact assessment. The local community living closest to the plant called on Sajudis and the greens to organize public hearings on the issues of Ignalina. It turned out that most people living close to the plant were unaware of the threats and risks they are facing.

In 1988, a petition with 44 thousand signatures was sent to the Prime Minister of the USSR with the request to stop the construction of the 3rd block or to change the type of reactor (Vaisvila, 1988). It also requested that inhabitants of Lithuania, Latvia and Belarus be informed about the operation of the plant and that there be an independent environmental impact assessment. As a response to this petition a letter was sent from the USSR Research Institute of the Exploitation of Nuclear Energy. Not surprisingly, it was stated in the letter that experts had analyzed the situation, considered the construction safe enough, and recommended to continue the construction of the 3rd reactor. (Lapienis, 1988). Thus, the public concern was expressed in a democratic way (letter or petition), and authorities responded in a formalist way (involvement of "experts", traditional conclusion that decision of authorities is correct from a scientific perspective). In a Western country this process would be regarded as a traditional kind of public-policy interface; however, this was a rather new experience of dialogue for public and policy makers in the former Soviet Union.

In September 1988, about 15,000 people inspired by the greens gathered at the Ignalina nuclear power plant, and the chain of people - "The Circle of Life" - surrounded the most dangerous site of the energy sector in Lithuania. This also inspired an action to collect signatures against the construction of the 3rd block. According to different sources, between 800 000 and 1.3 million signatures[7] were collected against Ignalina Nuclear Power plant during protest actions (Green Lithuania, 1992). This is probably the most significant figure illuminating the scale of public engagement in environmental science and technology policy in Lithuania.

Later on, the Lithuanian Government decided to stop the construction of the 3rd block, motivating it by the absence of comprehensive technical and environmental assessment. Thus, using various forms of public participation the greens achieved the result that construction of the 3rd block was terminated, and the management of the plant revealed ecological data to the public. This was quite a significant victory that demonstrated the capacity of public participation and its potential influence upon decision-making.

---

[7] Note that the total population of Lithuania is only 3.7 million.

5. Public Participation After the Restoration of Lithuania's Independence

The spring of 1989 can be regarded as a starting point of professionalization of the Lithuanian greens. During the first Congress of the Greens it was decided to establish the Lithuanian Green Party in order to have representatives in the Parliament (Supreme Council). The Green Party was established on July 15, 1989 and led by Zigmas Vaisvila. Since then the Green Movement and the Green Party functioned as two separate organizations. In March 1990, eleven people were elected to the Supreme Council representing yje Lithuanian Greens, among them were four members of the Green Party. However, it later turned out that green ideas and the authority of the greens was utilized by some people in order to get into the Parliament. Later some of those people discredited entirely the ideas and world views that the movement was promulgating, and although the Green party formally still exists, it does not have much in common with the ideas and platforms of counterparts in other European green parties.

The Green Movement had an immense social and political significance in 1988-1989,. However, the greens stopped their massive public actions after Lithuania declared its independence on March 11, 1990, and the USSR began its economic blockade. According to Linas Vainius, the current chairman of the Lithuanian greens, the future of Lithuania was uncertain politically and economically in 1990-1991, and therefore it seemed inappropriate to organize big ecological protest actions.

The new Lithuanian authorities were predominantly concerned with economics and politics, and paid little attention to environmental issues. A certain political bias in the way that the authorities were taking public opinion into consideration was increasingly noticeable as well. Therefore, according to the chairman of the greens, they decided to return to more activist and visible forms of protest and involvement in environmental science and technology policy (Martinkiene, 1995).

Because of the lack of tradition and experience in public participation, the involvement of NGOs and the public in the decision-making process was rather uneasy in this period. The legal system for public access to information, the public right-to-know, was underdeveloped. At the same time, the Government and local authorities were making (sometimes hindering) important decisions that created serious public concern. The two most significant examples were the case of hydro-accumulation power plant in Kruonis, and the municipal waste water treatment plant in Kaunas.

In the latter case, authorities were very slow to decide in which site the sewage treatment plant was to be constructed, while Kaunas was and still is considered the environmentally "hottest hot spot" in Lithuania[8]. Therefore, the greens led by their "soul" Saulius Gricius undertook quite publicly a drastic visible action: they organized a hunger strike in front of the building of the municipal authorities. This strike lasted several days until the authorities publicly announced that the site for Kaunas' water treatment plant had been selected. This can be regarded as a significant victory of the greens in influencing public decisions related to environmental technology. The site selection, however, has not been just an administrative decision catalyzed by the greens. Public discussions spread to other social groups - architects, land planners, civil engineers, local communities living in the neighborhood of the proposed site, and others. The actions of the greens and public debates in Kaunas gave an impulse and raised attention to other municipal environmental hot spots. Today, municipal waste water treatment plants are considered the first

---

[8] It is a major industrial city with nearly half a million inhabitants that does not have any kind of municipal waste water treatment facilities

priority in the National Environmental Strategy and Public Investment program of Lithuania. This fact can be viewed as having its roots in the active pressure and public mobilization by the Green movement in 1990-91.

The other case, the Kruonis' hydro-accumulation power plant, created an opposite opinion about the greens as the shapers of public policy, and general skepticism about public participation in policy-making. The greens strongly opposed the construction of this plant although it was very important for the development of the Lithuanian energy system. The new plant would technologically allow to even out the peaks of energy production between the day time when much more energy is needed for industry and households, and the night time. The greens questioned the environmental soundness of this project, argued that the continuous process of pumping up and down the water of Kaunas artificial lake would destroy irreversibly its ecological equilibrium. In order to stop the construction of this plant, the greens again undertook quite publicly a visible but also rather drastic action: they blocked the railway through which turbines had to be transported. The construction of the plant was suspended, and the new round of environmental assessment and public debates started. A study tour was organized for energy sector officials, municipal authorities, greens and other concerned parties to the two hydro-accumulation power plants in the neighboring Poland. It was demonstrated in this study tour that in practice such plants are not so environmentally harmful as was believed. The clouds of suspicion and public concern scattered, and construction of the plant at Kruonis renewed.

Unfortunately, the time that was spent for re-assessment and public debates was extremely costly. The construction of this plant was originally part of the five-year plan, and thus centrally funded by Moscow. After Lithuania declared its independence, many ties between Moscow and

Lithuania were broken, but not immediately - it was a gradual process. This also meant that although today particular ministries or committees in Moscow still transfer funds to Lithuania, they might not do so tomorrow. This was exactly the case of Kruonis plant: until the public consensus was reached that this plant is environmentally safe enough, Moscow stopped funding. It meant that the construction had to be further continued with internal funding from the scarce budget of Lithuania.

Today, the greens argue that their main message did not reach the public at the time they protested against Kruonis. Namely, this message was to not rush with Kruonis before it is not publicly decided about the future of Ignalina nuclear plant, because Kruonis was meant to become an integral part of electric energy system with Ignalina in its center. According to their chairman Linas Vainius, the greens admit this failure among the three main failures throughout the movement's existence (Lietuvos rytas, 1995.05.20)

The case of Kruonis is repeatedly mentioned as a negative example of public engagement in environmental science and technology policy. It is always taken as an example to illustrate that only "specialists" or "experts" should make decisions, and that public participation or participation of laymen is socially irrelevant and costly. This is also a rather controversial case illuminating contradictory values and world views. In the case of the third block of Ignalina, Lithuanian society seemed to be supportive of the precautionary principle, it opposed the view that only experts know the truth and are allowed to make decisions. On the other hand, Kruonis showed a rather contrary picture - many voices in society were disagreeing with a call for precaution and public scrutiny vis-à-vis the fact that it might cost financially much more than traditional way of decision-making.

This case is continuously recalled in recent debates on the construction of an oil terminal on the coast of the Baltic Sea. The latter case is probably the most illustrative in terms of debate on "public" versus "experts" in environmental science and technology policy making. It thus deserves to be analyzed in some detail.

6. The Oil Terminal on the Baltic Sea

Before discussing issues of public-policy interface, it is relevant to draw a contextual picture of the whole process. When Lithuania declared its independence, and Moscow started its economic blockade, the problem emerged for the country of how to secure alternative supplies of energy. Although Ignalina nuclear power plant produces about 90% of the electricity used in Lithuania, the supply of oil and natural gas is solely based on imports from Russia and CIS countries. The Government of Lithuania decided to construct an oil terminal thus assuring independence of country's energy sector and switching it over from the Russian energy supply system.

Lithuania has a terminal and special company for oil export in Klaipeda since 1959. However, this terminal was designed only for export, it was not suitable for import of oil products and by the late 1980s it was backward in all respects. Lithuania also has an oil refinery in Mazeikiai, the largest and most modern in the former USSR (built in the 1980s). Therefore, it was natural that already in the Soviet era it was planned to reconstruct the oil terminal in Klaipeda so that it would be suitable for the export of gasoline and other products made from Russian oil and refined in the company in Mazeikiai, Lithuania. Klaipeda terminal was designed for a much smaller export capacity than ministries in Moscow would like to export. In 1988-89, this terminal was used twice as much as its capacity allows, and therefore it raised understandable public anxiety and concern, particularly about potential oil spillage and fires.

The first pickets by greens began in May, 1989. However, as the director general of Klaipeda Oil company pointed out, the greens were intentionally catalyzed by the company to protest, because they were very popular at that time, and the company expected that in such a way it would be easier to convince bureaucrats in Moscow that the oil terminal needed reconstruction and additional finance (Lietuvos rytas, 1994.01.04). After massive public pickets even the Minister of the Oil and Gas Industry of the former USSR, Mr. Chernomyrdin[9], visited Klaipeda. The consensus was reached, one outcome of which was a commitment of the Prime Minister to allocate 90 million USD for reconstruction and development of Klaipeda Oil company. If it is true that the company intentionally involved and exploited greens for attracting the attention of high-ranking public policy makers, this might be qualified as a staining of the very idea of democratic public participation in decision-making in the name of the environment. We intend to further investigate this peculiar case of public-policy interface in the future.

Later, various options for reconstruction of the oil terminal were proposed: from developing the company on the same site to moving part of it to other sites on the Baltic coast. All options proposed had advantages as well as disadvantages, and the site selection for the oil terminal created unprecedented public debates in Lithuania. The main parties involved in the discussions were the Supreme Council (later the Parliament) of Lithuania, the Government represented by various ministries and individuals, local authorities of the city and district of Klaipeda, and local greens organization. Although all parties agreed that the oil terminal is a priority for Lithuania, nobody wanted to have it in

---

[9] Currently, the Prime Minister of Russia.

their "backyard". The authorities of the city of Klaipeda aimed to move the terminal further out of the town area. The motives were based on environmental, fire safety and other considerations, perceived as a threat to the city and its people. However, the whole coastal area is only 38 kilometers long (1 cm for every inhabitant of Lithuania!), and the attempts to suggest different sites outside the city of Klaipeda met resistance by the authorities of the District of Klaipeda and the authorities of Palanga, Lithuania's major health resort on the Baltic Sea coast. A great number of well-known Lithuanian artists and intellectuals communicated their opinion in the mass media. The Klaipeda oil company and representatives of municipal or district authorities all were looking for the parties in the central Government and Supreme Council to support their position. One example of such networks is the fact that resolution written by representatives of Klaipeda District and Palanga city with minor editions was shaped into a decisive letter signed by 46 members of the Supreme Council (Parliament).

Later it was revealed that in one area suggested for the oil terminal the authorities of Klaipeda were planning to build exclusive houses, cottages, and summer houses, in another area there were summer houses of representatives of the Ministry of Construction and Urban Planning, and yet at a third area suggested for the oil terminal there were summer houses of the Ministry of Energy. Thus, in all discussions "objective" environmental concern was mixed with personal or group vested interests.

To make the site selection procedure more neutral and "objective", the Danish company Knudsen-Soerensen was hired. Some parties regarded the pre-feasibility study made by this company as a trustworthy baseline for further research and design, whereas other parties criticized this study on different merits. Some argued that the site which the Danes supported was unacceptable because 200 hectares of unique forest planted in sand on the coast of the Baltic would be cut (Astravas, in Terminalas ant

Baltijos kelio, 1993). Others argued that those who contracted the Danish company for making the assessment already knew in advance which site would be suggested. It was said that assessment by a third party was made in order to hide the fact that the ministries and research institutes in Russia were standing behind all this project. Moreover, it was argued that the main objective was not to create an alternative way to import foreign oil into Lithuania, but to modernize facilities to export Russian crude oil, i.e., a continuation of the plans that were born years ago.

The Green movement tried to mediate and catalyze dialogue between various entities within the bureaucratic domain. In June 1991, the Greens suggested to the Lithuanian Government an alternative to the construction of a new oil terminal on the coast. They proposed to explore the possibilities to use facilities of an already existing oil terminal in Ventspils, a harbor in neighboring Latvia. This alternative was supported by some Lithuanian and foreign experts as well as by the Latvian officials (Terminalas ant Baltijos kelio, 1993). Nevertheless, the government finally decided to start the construction in a suburb of Klaipeda which was used for recreation. People living in Klaipeda and the local association of greens in Klaipeda organized protest actions calling on the Government to start negotiations with Latvia. Members of the City council of Klaipeda refused to endorse the governmental decision to place the terminal on the territory of the city. The response of the government to the public anxiety was the order of the Prime Minister (11 May 1992) on the use of police when needed with regard to the construction of the oil terminal in Klaipeda (Terminalas and Baltijos kelio, 1993).

A campaign against the Greens was initiated in the mass media. The Latvian side was accused of being unwilling to negotiate. This is probably the most repressive and undemocratic response to public pressure since the re-establishment of independent Lithuania. Nevertheless, the greens still tried to act as mediators between various parties within the bureaucratic domain. In Autumn 1992, representatives of the Greens visited the Supreme Council of Latvia. They found out that on the contrary, it was the Lithuanian side that showed no attempts to really explore other more environmentally friendly technological options and possible cooperation between the two countries. As a response to this visit the Greens received a letter from the Ministry of Energy informing them that a commission for negotiations with Latvia was formed. At the beginning of 1993, an economic, technical and environmental assessment of the Ventspils alternative was made, and this alternative was publicly rejected by the Lithuanian authorities as economically not viable.

Less officially, another explanation was circulating. The energy policies in Lithuania and Latvia are influenced by strategic decisions of official authorities as well as shadow economic parties in Russia. Both countries, Latvia and Lithuania, experience tough pressure from the big neighbor. It is argued that there are forces in both Lithuania and Latvia which represent the vested interests of oil and gas companies in the CIS, and the globalizing economy in this case is mixed up with the globalizing political issues (confrontation vs stability) and criminal issues (mafia). Thus, the fact that development of a complex cooperation between Lithuania having an oil refinery and Latvia having an oil terminal was blocked is explained by different parties as an outcome of external influences rather than an environmentally or economically grounded choice of authorities of the two countries. As a consequence, "... instead of mutually beneficial co-operation between two sister-countries we risk a chain of industrial hot spots along the Baltic Sea coast" (Povilanskas, 1993).

The intensive public debates encouraged the Government to take a step which was rather new in Lithuania in resolving public disputes. In early 1993, three different groups of experts - economists, ecologists and social scientists - were commissioned by the Ministry of Energy to assess the conflicting options regarding the site of the oil terminal. All three commissions were formed from well-known scholars in their respective field, and it was believed that those experts would give the scientifically "objective" answer. All three commissions came to the same conclusion, and the site was finally selected in Butinge very close to the Latvian border. Nevertheless, there still are a lot of public doubts regarding the objectivity of assessment in this particular case as well as the procedure of assessment in general (it is termed *ekspertize* in Lithuanian). As one professor recently noted in the largest newspaper "the environmental minister once told me that he can get any results of assessment (ekspertize) he needs" (Lietuvos rytas, 1996.12.17) Thus, even three parallel assessment commissions did not add much credibility to the ways in which central government is making decisions of national importance.

The construction of the oil terminal finally started in 1995, but tensions still did not slow down. The Klaipeda oil company in parallel continues its reconstruction, and thus creates an additional puzzle: what is the use of the entirely new oil terminal in Butinge if the Klaipeda terminal will be modernized and expanded? Which of the two is the one that will assure alternative import of energy resources independent from the supplies from CIS? The Ministry of Energy could not give any clear answer to these and other related questions. When trying to answer them one unwillingly returns to earlier indications that it is shadow economic interest groups rather than environmentally-informed and socially concerned authorities that are shaping the future of Lithuania's energy sector and oil business. This certainly has strong implications for the public-policy interface and institutional learning in this area of environmental and technological concern.

This case also illustrates the growing importance of local authorities vis-à-vis command from the central government As the former major of the City Council of Klaipeda, Mr. Ciapas, has pointed out:

Probably they would laugh in any other country of the world but Lithuania if they heard how the site for the oil terminal was initially chosen. One day there comes Mr. Simenas, (at that time chairman of the Nature Protection Commission of the Supreme Council), takes my car, and after some hours of driving around Klaipeda comes and says "Eureka, I found it!" I thought he was joking, but after a week the Government issued an order on the site for construction of the oil terminal...
(Terminalas and Baltijos Kelio, 1993:51)

On the other hand, when local authorities are opposing decisions made by central authorities, sometimes they do so not in order to find a solution to the problem, but to avoid this problem at their "backyard" and move it to other districts. This tendency can be observed not only in the case of the oil terminal, but also in other areas of environmental science and technology policy. It is visible in the recent case of site selection for a national hazardous waste management plant and in the project of disposal and incineration of old unused pesticides. In both cases, local authorities were extremely active trying to avoid environmentally risky industrial activities within the boundaries of their geographic location and jurisdiction. Although central authorities, e.g. the Ministry of Environmental Protection, took the initiative to carry out environmental assessment involving well-known scientists, this was not taken by the local authorities as sufficient. The main problem, however, was not the reliability and public credibility of environmental impact assessment, but the authoritative way in which the Ministry of Environment pushed along its decisions down to the municipal level.

In general, all these projects can be viewed as a sequence of lessons, a continuous process of learning of democratic decision making, and the making of an open society in Lithuania. The NIMBY syndrome is still prevailing, nevertheless, and often leads to what is called NIABY (Not In Anybody's Back Yard).

7. Conclusions

The rise of environmentalism in Lithuania and its influence upon science and technology policy in different ways resembles important features in the development of environmentalism in the Western countries. However, there are important differences as well. We will try to outline some of them by using a phase-wise analytical framework applied by Jamison for analysis of environmentalism in the Western countries (see introduction).

The rise of public environmental awareness in Lithuania took place in the relatively short period during 1988-89. As illustrated by some cases and examples presented in this paper, the period of public education can be characterized as a time of mobilization and social movement as well. The process of public environmental education in Lithuania often took place during significant public actions, for example rallies, which implies a parallel process of public mobilization and education. On the other hand, this rather spontaneous mobilization and up-swing of public environmental awareness is inter-linked with political controversy, questioning of particular science and technology options (Ignalina nuclear power plant, Kruonis hydro-accumulation power plant, etc.). The latter activities usually are attributed to the social movement phase in the development of western environmentalism.

Thus, there is no apparent time gap between those three processes that are portrayed in a phase-wise fashion in western environmentalism (cf Jamison et al 1990). However, the processes of public education (learning), social mobilization and movement can be distinguished as *qualitatively* important characteristics of environmentalism in Lithuania. The phase-approach is even more relevant for looking at the later development (professionalization and internationalization) of the environmental movement, starting from approximately 1990.

These processes were qualitatively quite distinct from the earlier period of environmentalism in Lithuania.

The contributions of academic institutions in public policy have still not diverged too far from the tradition rooted in the ideology of idealistic, "objective" science that was prevailing in the Soviet times. The culture of "expertise" dominates in most public debates over different issues of environmental science and technology policy. Usually, the governmental authorities rely upon authoritative academics and researchers (scientific statesmen) and use them as the unquestionable source of true knowledge in conflict situations. When the problems of public concern arise, authorities immediately form a group of experts who are supposed to carry out an objective assessment of the issues at stake.

Nevertheless, the cases are growing of public questioning of the "objectivity" of various kinds of assessment. The greens and other NGOs were most active in this process in the late 1980s and early 1990s, whereas currently local municipalities and other local authorities are becoming increasingly active in questioning various science and technology decisions. The most illustrative are the cases of the oil terminal on the Baltic Sea, and the case of incineration of unused pesticides in a fertilizers and a cement plant.

The future of the nuclear power plant in Ignalina still remains as a core issue of public concern around which the environmental science and technology policy discourse has developed. Public debates are not slowing down, on the contrary, they are growing and making a public space not just for discussing this particular area of public concern, but also the variety of social-economic and cultural-ethical questions concerning the future of the country and its people.

References

Beck U (1992). *Risk Society. Towards a New Modernity*. London: Sage Publications

Gineitiene D (1996) *The Role of the Lithuanian Green Movement in Decision Making*. Master's thesis. Kaunas University of Technology, Department of Public Administration

Gudavicius H (1988) *Issaugokime Lietuvos Dramblius. (Save Lithuania's Elephants)*. // Komjaunimo tiesa. 1988.10.18.

Green Lithuania (Zalioji Lietuva). Vilnius, 1992 May-June.

Jamison A., Eyerman R., Cramer J. (1990) *The Making of the New Environmental Consciousness: A Comparative Study of the Environmental Movements in Sweden, Denmark and the Netherlands*. Edinburgh: Edinburgh University Press

Januskis V. *Gamta ir Mes: Ekologines Problemos (Nature and Us: Ecological Problems)*.Vilnius: Mokslas, 1990.

Kalenda C (1992) *Ekologine Krize ir Dorove (Ecological Crisis and Ethics)*. Vilnius: Etines kulturos draugija "Ethos"

Karalius A (1990) Zalioji *Ideologija: Kodel Zalieji Zali (The Green Ideology: Why the Greens are Green)?* Kulgrinda. Nr.1.

Kavolis V (1994) *Samoningumo Trajektorijos (Trajectories of Consciousness)*. Zmogus istorijoje (Man in the history). Vilnius: Vaga

Kavolis V (1994) *Epochu signaturos (Signatures of Ages)*. Zmogus istorijoje (Man in the history). - Vilnius: Vaga

Kiek Gali Kainuoti Vieno Munduro Garbe (How Much Could the Honor Cost)? Vilnius: Literatura ir menas. 1986 11. 15.

Lapienis S. *Demesio ir Nerimo Centras (A Focus of Attention and Concern)*. Komjaunimo tiesa. - 1988.10. 06.

Law on Environmental Protection of the Republic of Lithuania.Environmental Protection in the Republic of Lithuania. Vilnius: Environmental Protection Department 1992. No.1.

Marcijonas, A (1978) *Teisine Gamtos Apsauga* (Legal Framework for Environmental Protection). Vilnius: Mintis

Martinkiene P. *Zaliuju Judejimas - Nepolitine Pilieciu Organizacija (The Green Movement is Non-Political Public Organization).* Vakaru ekspresas. - 1995.09.08.

Povilanskas R (1993) *Nafta - Kokia Kaina (Oil - at What Price)?* Terminalas ant Baltijos kelio (The Terminal on the Via Baltica). Vilnius: Zalioji Lietuva

Terminalas ant Baltijos kelio (The Terminal on the Baltic Road). Vilnius: Zalioji Lietuva, 1993.

Valionyte D. *Bundanti Gamta (Awakening Nature)* Kaunas: Kauno diena. 1996.05.0 9.

Vaisvila Z. *Pabuskime Visi (Wake Up All of Us)* Komjaunimo tiesa. 1988.08. 27.

Worster D (1977) *Nature's Economy: A History of Ecological Ideas.* Cambridge: Cambridge University Press

Zemulis F. *Zaliuju Vadas Tvirtina, jog Zalieji Buvo, Yra ir Bus (The Leader of Greens Maintains that the Greens were, are and will be)* Vilnius: Lietuvos rytas. 1995.05. 20.

Zemulis F. *Pirmasis Lietuvos Gamtosaugos Vadovas Tapo Legenda (The First Lithuanian Environmental Chief Became a Legend)* Vilnius: Lietuvos Rytas. 1996.01.20.

The Uncompromising Ally: Environmental Policy in Iceland

by Örn D. Jónsson

1. Introduction

Iceland is greening as any other relatively well off nation on the globe: every time someone tanks up, an investment is made in tree planting. The buying of a plastic bag in the supermarket means participation in one or another erosion prevention program. A number of recycling programs have been initiated, some of which have been far more successful than expected. The farmers and fishermen have set their sights on sustainability, by certifying farm products according to ecological standards and by fisheries regulation. Reykjavik has on its agenda to become the cleanest city in the world and the government has issued a white paper on environmental issues.

The above examples could be taken as signs that Icelanders are in the forefront of ecological awareness and practice. Such a statement would be at least boisterous, at worst silly. In matters where environmental issues are in direct conflict with economic interests, the latter usually have the upper hand. Pollution from factories is continuously visible, overgrazing is still tolerated and regulations of fisheries are limited to the 200 mile zone, whereas the tragedy of the commons reigns beyond that zone. Reykjavik has four or five times higher car-driven miles per capita than most cities of similar size in Europe. The situation here is that the diverse ideas concerning environmental issues have merged into one, nearly universal, paradigm of sustainable development. The general acceptance of a single environmental paradigm has been more or less taken for granted on the discursive level, which in turn has meant that a range of conflicts of interpretation and practice now occur within that paradigm. The present situation is somewhat reminiscent of what Herbert Marcuse and Robert P. Wolff criticised in the 1960s as *repressive tolerance* whereby a plurality of interests are treated on equal terms (cf. Marcuse et al 1969). On the policy level we have consensus, on the practical one, we enter the realm of conflicting interests.

This is not to say that divergence of opinion has disappeared. With the introduction of animal rights, the shift of the pendulum is nearly complete. Instead of regarding nature as servant of man's needs or longings, man is now requested to become nature's servant. This means that the Cartesian division between man and nature is upheld but with opposite polarities: now nature comes first. As Finn Lynge (1992: 13, 14)) has pointed out, "…rights are intimately connected with duties. If you have a human right to democracy, then you also have an obligation - a moral obligation, not necessarily a juridical one - to behave democratically yourself. If you have the right to know the truth, you also have the duty to be truthful yourself." He also points out that "no whale can exhibit 'unwhaley behaviour' - not even a killer whale."

In order to clarify our own standpoint, it might be useful to present a few assumptions and "stylised facts:"

1. The basic standpoint is a materialistic one. Man is a part of nature or of his own (human) nature (cf. Schmidt 1971).

2. "Pure nature" untouched by man has ceased to exist quite some time ago. Just as the anthropologist Levi Strauss (1973) didn't find primitive or untouched societies in his recollection of his stay in Brazil, the untouched environment became a myth well before the turn of the century.

3. The scale and scope of man's impact on nature has increased dramatically since the Industrial Revolution. The transformation of nature in the last four or five generations can be said to be more than the effects of all attempts of domestication from the beginning of human history. In the words of Victor Papanek (1995):

> The world we understand goes back only to the Renaissance. The world as we really know it dates back to the Industrial Revolution, and the world we feel comfortable with probably began - depending on our age and feeling for history - sometime between 1945 and 1973.

4. As Jamison (1996) puts it, "The contemporary concern with environmental problems is due to the scientific research ... it seems fair to say that scientists have constructed these problems, and not just any scientists, but particular cadres of well-supported and highly technified natural scientific researchers." This does not mean that scientists "invented" pollution, but rather scientific research laid the cornerstones for formulating environmental concerns into political issues postulated by interest groups as well as governmental agencies.

5. Environmental issues have developed from a concern formulated by social thinkers and natural scientists, to organised dissent by "single

issue groups" to a ruling paradigm postulated by public officials and professionalised non-governmental organisations alike.

6. "Taken in the context of our high-consumption, marketing-orientated, capitalist society, the 'Green consumer' is - almost invariably - first and foremost a consumer, and only nominally Green." (Whitely 1993) This may sound pessimistic, but we take it to mean that green issues in the context of consumption must, to a considerable extent, be adapted to dominant modes of behaviour.

To sum up: environmental issues have their roots in the increasing impact of man's domestication or exploitation of natural resources, especially in the industrialisation process. The sheer scale and scope of these activities have led to a shift in the discourse about the environment and to a lesser extent a change in praxis. The irreversibility of this process has become obvious and its seriousness has transformed the search for possible remedies from radical critique to tasks for which the ruling agents are to held responsible. The general public is prepared to stretch an arm but not a leg when it comes to environmental issues.

2. Development in Iceland - from a populist to an open market economy

If the concept of embeddedness or "organisational dependency" (Jonsson 1996) is to have a meaning, the specificity of the development in each country has to be accounted for. Iceland is a micro state, populated by 260 000 people geographically situated on an island of 103 000 square kilometers. It became a nation-state under the second world war and from an economic point of view should be regarded as a "late developer" heavily dependent on natural resources, primarily fisheries.

Until the second world war the economy could be said to be relatively closed, not by choice but rather by the extended duration of the world crises, prolonged by the collapse of the fisheries exports to Spain due to the civil war, which was the main market for salted cod in the inter-war years. The political system, as well as the institutional arrangement of the economy, took shape. Each class had its political party and the economy acquired strong populistic traits. Populism is used here in a value neutral sense, to refer to an economic system where the small entrepreneur is favoured over "big" industry and advancements through "simple production" are preferred to "economies of scale". Such a system needs a strong state and, instead of finance capital, money was redistributed through politically steered mechanisms (Jonsson 1985). Understanding this populistic economy of the inter-war years is crucial to our insights into the subsequent development. Economic issues, as well as environmental ones, were seen as a natural part of politics, both on a national and local level. The paternalistic role of the state was taken for granted by all actors, until fairly recently, if not in the political discourse, then in practice.

The state could allocate half of the income accumulated by the exports of fish under the second world war, it was the state that initiated negotiation around establishing an energy intensive industry in Iceland as well as the enlargement of the fisheries zone in steps, to 12 miles, 50 miles and finally to 200 miles. The enlargement was fought for by the state, and the shift in the role of the Marine Research Institute from exploring new fishing grounds to regulatory functions was based on governmental measures. With some simplification it can be stated that the political institutions took shape well before independence in 1944, but the actual construction of a modern market economy only started in the post war years gaining full force in the sixties and seventies. Early in the sixties a decision was made to join EFTA, although the actual membership didn't take shape until the beginning of the 1970s.

Today, the Icelandic economy can be said to be moulded in the same form as other OECD economies of similar stature, where its populistic origins time and again show up in politics and economic policy. The fact remains that Iceland is a micro society. Politics and, for that matter, economic change, has until recently drawn its stimulus from the civil society, i.e., the same social institutions that single issue movements have come from in larger societies. This has meant that formulated interests have been politicized quite easily or even institutionalized on a governmental level without significant conflicts. And this, in turn, means that the undergrowth of opinion building leading to counter movements, or NGOs, has been relatively limited. A clearly stated issue becomes a political one in the public debate and henceforth a part of the system. The same applies to such matters as science policy. Here a single person, or a small group, can have a great impact as long as it does not interfere drastically with the interests of a major societal group or economic interest.

3. The Building of a National Environmental Science Policy

As a general point of reference, Jamison has characterized the phases of post-war environmentalism in terms of five main periods (see introduction).

Although the periodisation can be applied to the development in Iceland, it has its specific traits as in other countries. The main divergence can be said to be threefold.

- Due to the sparse population and the populistic characteristics the relative importance of civil society is greater in Iceland than in many other countries. For the same reason the interconnectedness between the civil society and the social institutions such as the bureaucratic, economic and political has also been more detectable.
- There is a time lag. Measures regarding environmental issues that were taken in the early seventies in the neighbouring countries only materialised in Iceland in the late eighties.
- Due to harsh living conditions close to the arctic, and the relative dependence on exploitation of natural resources, an abstract conception of nature is close to inconceivable. Man, in his daily struggle for existence, is a part of nature, a nature that gives and takes. Concerns with over-exploitation have been closer to the heart of the general public as well as scientists than the overall, and often ill detected, consequences of the globalisation of the industrialisation process.

A policy related to environmental matters started to crystallise in the early 1970s as in most other countries, although the issue can be traced back to the beginning of the century, or even earlier. Laws concerning animal preservation were set in 1887, in 1894 laws determining the conservation of forests were set and in 1928 specific areas were preserved by law (Guttormsson1974).

As a part of the fight for national independence, a certain vision of unspoiled nature emerged, based on a glorified picture of the settlement process. Iceland, a barren, mountainous, rocky island, was envisaged as fertile and covered with trees from the shores to the mountain tops. It became a part of the rituals of the *Youth Society* to plant trees, and this symbolic action has been the basis for a persistent myth of environmental concern; planting symbolises growth, the ability of man to revive the past glory and start anew, as a kind of "concrete utopia".

In 1956 preservation laws where presented for the parliament and accepted, thirteen years later, or in 1969, new laws were passed that gave the *Náttúruverndarrádi* (or the Nature Conservation Society) a considerable mandate on environmental issues. It is important to stress that, although the society partly had the status of an NGO it was from the outset financially supported by the government. The main reasons for awakening of environmental interests was increasing scientific knowledge, and the obvious consequences of rapid technological development, whereby pollution, the over-exploitation of ecological systems, and the destruction of natural reserves by unchecked use of machinery. Natural scientists were in the forefront of this awakening, influenced by the surge of environmental concerns abroad.

In 1969 the Youth Society (an organisation dating back to the first decade of the century, that has very minimal resemblance with the youth movements in other countries) held a conference on nature conservation and the dangers of erosion. Four years earlier, Rachel Carson's book, *Silent Spring* had been translated, and there was a growing number of people, educated abroad, who raised issues concerning over-exploitation and pollution. But although the main impetus came from the combination of foreign influence and the increasing number of natural scientists, conflicts around land use accelerated this process. It reminded Icelanders that they were a part of the global trend of the increasing vulnerability of the environment to human activities. The farmers' fights against the building of a hydroelectric power station at Laxá, a river in the north of Iceland, triggered off harsh disputes about land use and national priorities. The local farmers won and the conflict set an example influencing subsequent disputes, even outside the national borders as in the EEC conflict in Norway: as a classic tale of David and Goliath.

Although these movements emerged at the same time as the youth movements in Europe and USA it would be a bad case of historical rewriting to assume that the conservation movements had much in common with the rebellious movements abroad. The '68 generation in Iceland was engulfed in a kind of neo-nationalism, fighting American imperialism, symbolised by the NATO base in Keflavik, and even, occasionally, the atom bomb and the Vietnam war. The environment was not an issue for these groupings, apart from some "hippies" that established one or two communes outside the Reykjavik area.

It is here appropriate to discuss the specificity of the situation in Iceland. Scientists and laymen could organise themselves around nature conservation. But any romantic regression to a former state of harmony between man and nature was impossible. Icelanders, like any other people living on the verge of the nearly inhabitable arctic, have learned to respect nature, as a force that gives and takes. The most common view of nature is that of a demanding friend. The harsh winters a few years ago with catastrophic avalanches in the western fjords certainly affirmed this Janus-faced attitude to nature.

The persons that under other circumstances would have established idealist movements could organise themselves in semi-governmental institutions that were financed, or partly financed, by the state. The price for such an arrangement was probably a loss of distance or critical standing, but instead the concerned persons, mostly natural scientists, could have direct influence on legislation . The same persons would pop up in different contexts, both nationally and internationally, sometimes representing the government sometimes not. In a sense this makes the system unusually transparent but also open to nepotism.

This is probably part of the explanation behind the decision not to establish a Ministry of Environment in the wake of the Stockholm conference in 1972. The issue was taken up in the Parliament in 1973, but only resulted in a revision of the laws concerning environmental conservation. The NCS functioned, albeit in a problematic way, as the Ministry of the Environment. The ministry was first established in 1990.

If we look at the development in Iceland in the light the periodisation presented earlier, the development can be said to follow the general pattern until the early 1970s. The issues were raised and discussed, but subsequent institution building that took place in most European countries in the wake of the Stockholm conference only partly took place in Iceland. The environmental conflicts that arose were primarily related to land use and, of course, the concern for the over-exploitation of the fishing grounds. As the fisheries were not limited to Icelandic vessels, the attempt to regulate the effort in the commons became a nationalist issue: a fight for a national monopoly to utilise the fishing grounds around Iceland. The fisheries zone was enlarged to 50 miles and later to 200 miles. Questions around pollution were raised, but not taken seriously by the majority of the population.

4. Emerging Policy and Conflicts of Interest

Nature is obviously the primary source of wealth for the population in Iceland. Up until the second world war concerns about fisheries were voiced by the advocates of farming. Fisheries were regarded as a secondary preoccupation, while modernisation of land use should be the primary focus for the Icelandic population.

> ...in the present situation in this country it is highly
> dangerous for people in the rural areas or smaller
> communities to move to the towns. ... the nation
> will gain its strength by living off the land in a self
> sufficient manner, where the homespun ingenuity
> will be the main source of prosperity" (Jónas frá
> Hriflu1935)

This kind of view, here expressed by one of the leading politicians at
that time, dignifying self-sufficiency was not uncommon in the 1930s.
The influx of capital, new technology and modern consumerism in the
wake of the second world war made such views strangely outdated, but
the efforts to harness nature and make it a servant of man were
universally accepted, until fairly recently. Nature hardly had a voice of
its own, so to speak. The main occupation of scientists and technicians
was finding ways to extract increasing economic value from natural
resources. First from the land and then from the sea, institutions were
built around this endeavour, at first related to the University of Iceland
and then as independent governmentally related agents co-ordinated by
the National Research Council which was created in 1965.

Environmental concerns were built into these institutions from the
outset. In the 1983 review of science policy by the OECD, the aims of
the National Research Council (NRC) and the technology support
institutions are presented. Of the five main objectives one deals with the
environment:

> Improved co-existence of land and people by
> protecting the natural environment, by improving
> the man-made environment and by broader and
> better planned utilisation of the Icelandic natural
> resources (OECD 1983).

The main objective of the Marine Institute was "to derive the optimal
contribution of the fisheries to the economy." But this was to be done

in a responsible manner: "To ensure maximum sustainable yield from Icelandic fish stocks and other living resources of the sea in the long term" and "To adjust fishing effort and fishing technology to prevent harmful consequences on the ocean bio-systems."

Even the Fisheries Research Laboratories whose main aim was to improve productivity and introduce quality measures voiced environmental concern, but in a peculiar way: "To combat negative environmental effects and to improve facilities at the workplace." Similar objectives were set for the Agricultural Institute. This in turn meant that the Natural Science Institute, which can trace its history back to 1989, in practice took on the role of a museum outside the practical or economic sphere. (Ottoson 1994) In the 1960s the University of Iceland started to expand rapidly. Faculties in natural science and earth sciences were set up and became quite popular. The popularity was not only due to an increased interest in environmental issues, but also because of the growing need for specialised knowledge in various segments of society as well as the construction of energy intensive industry and, in general the modernisation of the Icelandic society. The students graduating from the University grew in number, from 350 in 1965 to over 1700 in 1990 to over 2000 in 1995.

To summarise: the "single issue movements" focusing on environmental issues that later developed into NGOs never gained ground in Iceland. But that is not to say that their influence was not felt. Due to the populistic nature of the economy and because politics drew on the civil society, just as the movements in other countries did, questions related to environmental protection were institutionalised quite early on. However there was a close linkage between the scientification of environmental issues and economic issues related to the exploitation of natural resources.

5. The Environmental Institutions

In the light of the relative size of the Icelandic society the structure of the institutions that deal, one way or another, with environmental issues is surprisingly complex. The formal science and research organisations were organised in the following manner in 1995 but are now being reconstructed:

Figure One:

Research Organisation in Iceland

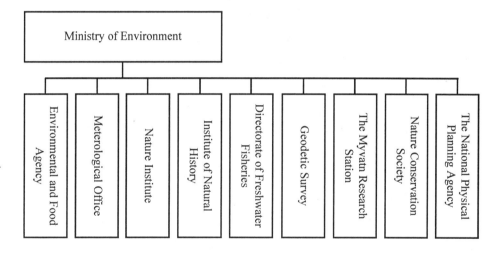

The two groups that were the most influential in shaping environmental policy at the outset were the farmers and the fishermen. The farmers' stake was related to land use. The populistic traits of the economy meant that there was a close inter-linkage between the entrepreneurial spirit that characterises economic activity and participatory involvement. This close connection between the economic and civil society also set the agenda for the institutionalisation of scientific involvement in relation to environmental issues. The Marine Institute was set up in order to facilitate utilisation of the resources of the sea, the Agricultural Institute's main objective was to increase productivity. Later on, when the target was set on building power plants, the Energy Institute was established. When environmental issues were set on the agenda these institutes were the natural agencies for taking care of such matters. This, in turn, meant that there was not perceived a need for a separate agency for environmental issues until quite recently. The Ministry of Environment was established in 1990, and reforms passed in the parliament in 1994-5 institutionalised the international agreements made in the wake of the UN conference in 1992, which gave existing institutes such as the National Planning Institute and the Nature Institute a new role. Here there can be said to be a change in emphasis, where the bureaucratic establishments with their emphasis on order and regulation come into the fore. In addition to these two aforementioned institutes, a third one was established in 1992-3, the Fisheries Institute, set up to regulate the utilisation of marine resources.

The picture that emerges is that of bureaucratisation of environmental issues, whereby the governmental institutes draw their legitimacy from international agreement and formal scientific knowledge rather than the interests of the economic or civil society. This arrangement is recent and only time will tell how it will fare. As yet no severe conflicts have arisen where economic or civil interests directly confront international agreements mediated by these governmental agencies. But it can be foreseen that the formal, the entrepreneurial and the participatory value systems will not thrive together in peaceful co-existence for ever.

6. Construction through Conflict

As the advocates of the social constructivist view of technology and science are apt to point out, the characteristics and evolution of these systems can best be studied through the conflicts that manifest themselves at the outset, or in the construction phase (cf. Bijker et al 1987). The guiding principle should be to "follow the actors". In the several conflicts that will be analysed here, concerning environmental and conservation issues it will become clear which interests were at stake and which group of actors stood behind them. These cases should not be regarded as an attempt to write the history of environmental awareness in Iceland, but rather as incidents that possibly throw light on how environmental concern has evolved in the postwar years, its changing scientific base, the actors involved and the making of policy related to the subject.

In the case of agriculture or land use the first emphasis was on the importance of self-sufficiency and although it could be deemed as an historical anachronism, self-sufficiency was regarded as synonymous with sustainability. The supporting measures were geared towards productivity, but on a small scale. The household farms were seen as the cornerstones, and as agricultural production expanded, conservation measures were taken, although often partly in conflict with the primacy of farming, or practical utilisation of land. This coincided with the aforementioned vision of paradise lost: it was acknowledged to a certain extent that sheep farming hindered the recapturing of the flourishing vegetation of the settlement years.

Increasing industrialisation and the building of the infrastructure led to conflict around land use. These conflicts concentrated around the decisions to construct power plants at various sites around the country. The first dispute around Laxá in the north of Iceland in the sixties and seventies set the agenda to a certain extent. Later, in the early eighties a bitter dispute occurred around Blanda, a power plant located in the north-west part of Iceland and to this day, for various reasons, there has not been an acceptable solution. Although this conflict did not have the same wide reaching political consequences as the confrontations around the Aardal and Sunndal Værk and later Alta in Norway, it can be said to have developed into a basic question about land use, and the crucial issue of ownership of the unpopulated areas of the country, or the commons.

The conflict around Blanda is a complex one. In the small local communities as well as in the Parliament there was a strong support for the construction of a power plant in the area. It was seen as an opportunity to revitalise the national and as well as the local economy. The opposition came from the local farmers who used two basic arguments for their cause. One was based on environmental conservation, the other on land use. The construction of the power plant meant that a considerable amount of fertile land went under water resulting in fundamental environmental changes in the natural habitat. This would not only change the flora of the area but also alter the conditions for fresh-water fish such as trout and salmon, of which the latter had a considerable economic significance for the locals (salmon fishing was the cornerstone of tourism in the area). Negotiations were undertaken where the main issue soon became the compensation for the land that went under water. This led to significant assessment processes where official experts, as well as some private engineering companies, were involved. The farmers organised themselves around the local Conservation Society, hitherto regarded as a threat to their interests. This can be interpreted as a major turning point in the relationship between the farmers and the government. As a part of the populistic order, local issues found a voice nationally and, in a sense, national policy was to a large extent a compromise between these local interests.

148

In the dispute around the *Blanda*, in the construction of the power plant, the state represents economic growth, and pursues its interests against the local community, the cornerstone of the former populistic system. The role of science was that of assessment and, later on, to regain the lost land in nearby arable areas.

To complicate matters, the government couldn't find buyers for the generated energy because of the global crises of the energy intensive sector. Furthermore the crises in farming and subsequent reduction of the sheep stock meant that the lost grazing areas became devoid of economic meaning. As the compensation terms were not agreed upon the conflict evolved into a farce like battle. The Minister of Industry had decided that monetary compensation was out of the question. Instead, the Agricultural Institute initiated the hitherto biggest project of cultivation in the highlands, joining forces with the Land Cultivating Institute (the state body that is to fight erosion). Over five hundred tonnes of fertiliser were flown from a nearby village every summer to the cultivation areas. The volatility of the endeavour was such that it was not suitable for grazing and, furthermore, the area needed continuous fertilisation. As one farmer in the area put it, the only party that has gained from this conflict are the wild geese in the highlands, as fences cannot keep them out of the fertilised areas.

After nearly 15 years, the conflict is still unresolved, the compensation now amounts to more than 10% of the construction costs of the power plant, and what is even more ironical, the small amounts that the farmers extracted from these considerable costs in monetary terms were to be invested in a hotel in one of the most popular nature resorts in the highlands. Here a new actor comes to the fore, the tourist or leisure industry. The building of the hotel was severely opposed by the *Travel Society,* backed by the tourist interests. In this context the influence of foreign NGOs can be detected. Nature should not be valued solely from a utilitarian standpoint, or rather leisure use of land is a legatee utilisation. The farmers, who historically have the utilisation rights of the highlands, have no right to monopolise these resources. The unpopulated areas of Iceland should be regarded as commons for all to enjoy in a responsible manner.

The picture that emerges in relation to land use is therefore quite complex. The actors involved are the developers of the "clean energy resources" of hydroelectical power. The farmers were now regarded as the biggest environmental threat through overproduction of lamb meat (a production heavily subsidised by the government). The leisure industry, which opposes both the over-exploitation of land and the environmental damage caused by the construction of power plants, backs up their claims by reference to the increasing significance of tourism as an economic activity. The leisure interests have even confronted the most enduring myths of utilitarian exploitation of natural resources. The poles carrying electricity are not a sign of man's harnessing the forces of nature, they are a "visual pollution" and planting trees and *lupina* to stop erosion is a questionable way of solving the serious problem of erosion because it affects biodivesity. In this view the emphasis should be on ways that do right to the spectacular beauty of the unpopulated areas. The policy should not be geared towards pseudo-domestication of the wilderness, but to preserve its uniqueness.

The disputes around land use have therefore swayed the environmental policy and its scientific components away from exploring more effective means of exploitation to conservation and environmental monitoring through assessment and preventive measures. The university researchers have actively contributed to this shift and the Agricultural Institute seems to be redefining its role in this direction. In mid-1996 an assessment project was initiated by the Ministry of Environment where these conflicting interests were set up as alternatives, but with the focus on the most constructive compromises. This project can be said to represent a major shift in environmental policy regarding land utilisation, irrespective of the outcome of the work.

If we turn to fisheries, the concerns there seem to revolve around the worries of over-exploitation of the resources of the sea, a concern that can be traced back to the turn of the century, but showed its full significance for Icelanders with the collapse of the herring stock in the 1960s. Here the relationship between technological innovation in searching and catching techniques and increased effort leading to over-exploitation was obvious. The subsequent increases in fishing other species than the traditionally commercial ones, which was facilitated by rapid advances in technology, evoked interest for a new regulating system. Quotas were introduced in the herring fisheries in 1965. TAC (Total Allowable Catch) was implemented in 1976, divided into individual vessel quotas. In 1979 these vessel quotas were made transferable. Similar vessel quotas were introduced in the chaplain fishery in 1980 and made transferable in 1986. Between 1989 and 1991 a comprehensive ITQ (Individual Transferable Quotas) system was implemented for nearly all other commercial species and it was developed into an all-encompassing system a few years later (Helgason 1991).

All major interest groups participated in building up of this system, and to a large extent this negotiation process was close of the procedures advocated by the adherents of "Constructive Technology Assessment" (cf Remmen 1995). Dialogue Workshops were set up, negotiating for more than a year. Although total consensus was not attained (where local opposition from the fishermen in the western fjords was the most prominent) the resulting system was accepted, since there seemed to be no viable alternatives.

The building of the quota system institutionalised a shift in the role of science concerning the utilisation of marine recourses. As the anthropologist Gísli Pálsson has argued, a radical shift in legitimacy took place. The fishermen had through the ages been primary exponents of the knowledge of the sea. The marine biologists came in as allies, aiding the fishermen in the search for new fishing grounds. As utilisation neared over-exploitation, the role of the scientists changed, from exploring to building a knowledge base for conservation or, to phrase it in modern terms, sustainable utilisation of marine resources. This eventually led to conflicts, where the quest for legitimacy and subsequent influence on political decisions concerning fisheries policy were debated. The tacit knowledge of the fishermen, grounded in practical experience confronted the formal knowledge acquired via scientific methods. This discourse was not purely economic, but was deeply rooted in civil society and the self-identity of the fishermen and consequently their occupational image. Fishing was regarded as an admirable practice, where fishermen staked their lives in order to exploit the riches of the sea. Advancements in technology had not only increased the efficiency of fisheries but also reduced the risk of the endeavour. The stage which now has been reached, where it is possible to fish any species, anywhere at any time, was clearly in sight in the late sixties and the beginning of the seventies. In the possession of such means the fishermen lost their "innocence". The need to restrict their efforts was clearly perceived by the general public. The scientists march to conquest was a conflict ridden one. The Marine Institutes advise on TAC's was at first taken as basic guideline for the politicians, which then took into consideration to other interests, usually exceeding the Marine Institutes recommendations by 15% to 20%. But in 1996 the scientists seemed to have conquered as the Fisheries Minister proclaimed that TAC should be restricted to the Institute's proposals. Or in his own words in a television interview: "Science rules".

This is not to say that the dispute has been laid to rest. The nearly total official hegemony of scientific advice has been questioned by the scientific community itself, and more and more crucial questions regarding the ecology of the sea are left open ended. But the principle of sustainability has been accepted by all the major players in the system and the basic rules of the discourse are derived from the findings of the scientists. Formal knowledge is accepted as the primary source, while the informal tacit knowledge of the practitioners of fisheries is slowly regaining ground, but as a secondary source. The obvious reason for this is the recurring failures in cod recruitment for more than ten years, leaving the most valuable stock in a vulnerable conditions. Or as one of the foreign advisors of fisheries policy, John Pope (1992), puts it, When the spawning stocks have reached such low levels, the ecological system should be given the benefit of the doubt.

Although the marine scientists and the fishermen have had prolonged arguments on policy matters regarding the utilisation of marine resources they have joined forces against the environmental NGOs on the issue of whaling. Here their understanding of sustainability is agreed upon: sustainable utilisation of the resources should encompass all species. There are no animals in the ecosystem that have specific rights, which is a view that advocates responsibility, but can at times turn into fierce attacks on species that are regarded harmful for the most valuable commercial species, as in the case of the seal. For several years a war was waged on the seal because of its role in the life chain of a parasite found in fish. But generally this view can be regarded as a responsible interpretation of sustainability, more in accord with its general rules than that of the NGOs that give one species priority over others. The commercial exploitation of the whales has been held back by the overall commercial interests of the fishing industry. If whaling should be started again it would probably damage the image of Icelanders as a fisheries nation, and henceforth ruin some of the most valuable markets.

A recent incident points in the direction that general attitudes are changing. A whale got stuck on a reef. In the case of similar incidents few years ago the first reaction was to utilise it, but here, although this happened in a fisheries dependent community, the locals first reaction was to free the animal and steer it back to the sea, a kind of "free Willy" effect!

The last case is that of the energy sector. As stated earlier the conflicts of power plants triggered off disputes about land utilisation. But, at first, these conflicts could be interpreted as economically related rather the environmental disputes. In the wake of the oil crises electric power generated by harnessing of waterfalls became regarded as 'clean energy production' and, as such. a feasible alternative to the use of non-renewable fossil resources. But the interests of the numerous multinationals that saw Iceland as a favourable location for their plants could be seen as an attempt to find areas where laws concerning environmental regulations were not as strict as in the neighbouring countries. At least ten of the sixty feasibility studies for energy intensive industry to be located in Iceland indicated that the main reason for the choice of location was a search for less restrictive environmental regulations. Icelandic scientist, mainly engineers and technicians seem to have shown little concern for the polluting effects of these projects. Their primary interest, reflected in the general economic policy, has been to find ways to create new jobs through utilisation of electric power on a large scale.

7. Concluding Remarks

Environmental issues have been, at the same time, central and peripheral in the Icelandic discourse. The issues concerning conservation and prevention of over-exploitation of the natural resources have been in the foreground. Concerns related to pollution or the more abstract aspects of mans exploitation of natural resources have been relatively peripheral. Topics like global warming, the thinning of the ozone layer and polluting effects of pesticides like TNT or substances like PCP have been debated, but it was not before the undersigning of the RIO tract that such matters were integrated into the bureaucratic system, backed up by political legislation. The NGO's that grew out the grass root movements in the sixties and seventies never got a foothold in Iceland. Partly because some of the major issues of these movements were seen as damaging for the nations interests, such as whaling, and now universal rules around restrictions on fisheries. And, partly, because the actors, that otherwise would have been the creators of these movements, integrated themselves or were integrated into the political system or formed semi-governmental pressure groups. A third aspect should be mentioned. The close links between the political and civil society on the one hand and the interconnections between the scientific community and the economic interests embodied in the Technology Support Institutions and the University. The influence of the grass root movements, and later on the NGO's, seem therefore to have been indirect, through the studies of Icelandic scientists abroad and through international agreements. The latter factor seems to be gaining importance as new governmental institutions are being built around these international agreements. The Nature Institute, and its new role, is an embodiment of these new times. Whether or not the new green bureaucrats will set the agenda remains to be seen. But the merging role of civil society seems to just as much regressive or the defence of short term local interests as progressive in the meaning of taking a responsible global view. If this turns out be the case a strange polarisation of roles has occurred in Iceland, and for that matter, possibly elsewhere.

References

Á leid til sjálfbærrar Thróunar (1993) Umhverfisráduneytid, Reykjavík.

Bijker, W.E., Hughes, T.P., Trevor, P. (1993) *The Social Construction of Technological Systems, New Directions in the Sociology and History of Technology*, The MIT Press, Massachusetts.

Brátt hafist hand vid gerd flugvallar á Blondusvaedinu, Feykir 30.6.1993

Carson, R. (1965) *Raddir vorsins thagna, Almenna* bókafélagid, Reykjavík

Guttormsson, H. (1974) *Vistkreppa og náttúruvernd*, Mál og menning, Reykjavik

Helgason, Th. (1991) *The Icelandic Quota Management System, A Description and Evaluation*, University of Iceland.

Jamison, A. (1996) "The Shaping of the Global Environmental Agenda: The Global role of Non-Governmental Organisations," in S Lash, et als, eds, *Risk, Environment and Modernity,* Sage Publications, London.

Jonsson, I. (1996) *Reflexive Modernisation, Organisational Dependency and Global Systems of Embedded development - a Post Colonial view*, Gronlandsk kultur & samfundsforskning, 95/96, Ilisimatusarfik, Nuuk

Jonsson, O.D.(1985). *Paa Sporet af den Populistiske Economy*, Roskilde University Center, Roskilde

Jónas frá Hriflu, Tíminn, 16 apríl, 1935.

Lynge, F. 'Ethics of a Killer Whale', in *Whales and Ethics*, ed. Jonsson, O.D. (1992) Fisheries Research Institute, University of Iceland, Reykjavík

Marcuse, H. et al (1969) *A Critique of Pure Tolerance*, Cape Edition, London.

OECD(1983) *Review of National Science Policy of Iceland*, OECD, Paris, p.73.

Ottoson, J.G. *Natturufraedistofnun Islands*, Arsrit 1994, p 5.

Palsson, G. (1991) *Coastal Economies, Cultural Accounts*, Manchester University Press, Manchester.

Papanek, V. (1995) *The Green Imperative, Ecology and Ethics in Design and Architecture,* Thames and Hudson, Singapore.

Pope, John. (1992) *Assessment of the Marine Institute*, Unpublished manuscript.

Remmen, A. (1995) "Pollution Prevention, Cleaner Technologies and Industry," in A Rip, et al, eds*, Managing Technology in Society.* Pinter Publishers, London.

Schmidt Alfred, (1971) *The concept of nature in Marx*, NLB, London

Strauss, C.L.(1973) *Tristes Tropiques*, Penguin, Harmondsworth

Whitely, N.(1993) *Design for Society*, Reaction Books, London.

Public Participation in Environmental Science and Technology:
The Dutch National Experience, 1960s-1990s[10]

by J.M. Andringa and J.W. Schot

1. Introduction

Since the mid-1960s public participation in environment and technology issues has developed in various ways. In this period, technology policy emerged as a separate activity distinct from both science policy and industrial policy. A new environmental technology policy is currently emerging. It is not an explicit, well-defined policy field, but rather one that is composed of several related fields. To understand this development, we will trace the various forms of public participation and of the involved policy fields in the current policy from the mid-1960s onward. We have divided this short history of environmental technology policy into three periods: from about 1965 to 1974; from 1975 to 1985; and from 1986 to now. In each period we show how the emerging environmental technology policy was derived from handling important environmental, technological and public issues.

At present, the most important actor in technology as a general policy issue is the Ministry of Economic Affairs. The emerging environmental technology policy, especially with respect to the supply side of environmental technology, is part of this general technology policy. Some

---

[10] We are indebted to Tom Misa for copy editing.

other ministries do make some technology policy, directed to their specific concerns. These technology policies are diffuse, however, and mostly derive from questions in the specific areas. Most attention is given to the demand side of environmental technology. Three other ministries have high levels of involvement: the Ministry of Housing, Planning and the Environment; the Ministry of Transport, Public Works and Water Management; and the Ministry of Agriculture, Nature and Fisheries. The latter two ministries will receive little attention in this paper, but they may play a larger role in later phases of our research.

2. Discussions on 'quality of life', 1965-74

During the period from World War II to the mid-1960s, the Dutch economy was built up and technology seemed promising. The post-war political climate was rather stable, with little apparent discontent. People concentrated on the goal of rebuilding the country as quickly as possible. Government intervention in (re-)building and the large general demand for goods stimulated by the population explosion after the war were two important factors in the rapidly shifting economic situation of the Netherlands (Jamison et al. 1990: 124, 125).

Through the mid-60s Dutch society was characterised by a segmentation into various religious or political blocs, called 'pillarisation'. Pillars, or groups, united people not only with respect to religious and political issues, but also to practically every sphere of social life (cf. Goudsblom, 1967). The members of these groups who were involved in political decision-making were used to a political attitude of making compromises and trying to settle differences of opinion in a spirit of co-operation and mutual benefit.

From the mid-60s onwards the consensus that typified the post-war period collapsed. The Dutch began to criticise the existing power structures in society and to demand different forms of political participation and democratisation. They attacked the policy of accommodation and pacification and wanted to break through the traditional organisation of society with its well-defined, fixed roles. The call for democratisation went hand in hand with a distrust of the established institutions, including traditional political parties. A process of rapid secularisation and de-pillarisation followed. This process broadened the political field and allowed extra-parliamentary groups to arise.

These extra-parliamentary groups were not entirely new, but their rapid appearance and the issues they raised were unusual. A leading issue was 'quality of life' including environmental degradation. Several environmental action groups emerged from these concerns. They had broad characteristics in common: they criticised economic growth as a dominant goal for society, and they had a distinct way of directing the attention of government and industry to pollution problems. They tried to mobilise public opinion by means of *ad hoc* symbolic actions, by writing popular articles in newspapers, distributing pamphlets, collecting signatures and organising hearings. They also broadcast large-scale television programmes, a new media at that time, to direct the attention of a broader public to pollution problems.

A highlight in the discussions about 'quality of life' and environmental matters was the appearance in 1972 of *Limits to Growth,* a report of the Club of Rome. The book fed the public feelings of discontent, predicting that population and production growth would be limited in the near future by the scarcity of food and natural resources. Few books of this type were available at the time, and the report referred and contributed to the general discussions. Nowhere was the 'limits to growth' thesis so widely discussed as in the Netherlands. Accordingly public concern on environmental problems grew quickly. Cramer points to the early 1970s as the period of 'environmental consciousness-raising' (cf. Jamison et al 1990). Opinion polls in 1970 showed that 71% of the Dutch population 'strongly agreed' and an additional 25% 'agreed' with the statement that the government should take severe measures to control environmental pollution.

Environmental groups were critical of technologies. They pointed to the various detrimental effects of specific technologies, including pollution, decreasing employment, and labour conditions. Especially criticised was the large scale on which technologies were applied. Most environmental groups did not offer alternatives for the technologies they criticised. In this regard the so-called Provos are an exception. The Provos developed several 'white plans' to explore alternatives. An example is the 'white bike plan' in which they proposed that the municipality of Amsterdam would buy 20,000 white bikes every year in order to extend public transportation in the city. Everybody could use these bikes, but they could not be claimed as one's own.

Although attention was directed to environmental and social problems, a general tendency can be seen, moving from criticism of *specific* technologies in the beginning of this period to criticism of technologies' effects on society *in general* (Smits and Leyten 1991: 68). The 'limits to growth' thesis implicitly questioned unlimited technological development, too. A white paper, called 'Selective Growth', was jointly produced in 1976 by the ministries of Economic Affairs, of Financial Affairs, and of Social Affairs. It was a response to these critical discussions of rapid technological developments.

A controversial technology that became important in the Netherlands in the early 1970s was nuclear energy. In 1973-74 the Dutch government decided to build more nuclear power stations. At the same time electricity prices were raised by 3% to contribute to building the nuclear reactor in Kalkar (Germany). In the beginning only environmental action groups made a stand against nuclear energy. Later on citizen protests increased, resulting in some large protest actions at the end of the decade.

In the late 1960s the knowledge interests of the action groups were diffuse. The broad diversity of people involved in these groups, the attention to specific cases of pollution instead of the fundamental causes, and the absence of publications on environmental-related themes all contributed to a lack of focus in developing an environmental knowledge base. In the early 1970s the knowledge interests of environmental groups became at once more specific and more divergent. Some groups were grass-roots organisations who developed alternative knowledge outside traditional sciences; others relied heavily on scientific expertise. (A similar divergence can be seen towards technological knowledge.) The general atmosphere of tolerance and pluralism in the Netherlands made it possible for all these different groups to exist and act in their own specific way, without a need to define or explicate common features.

A general tendency in the political sphere was the desire to break through traditional structures. Many people wanted to get rid of centralised structures. They asked for decentralisation of decision-making and more possibilities for participation. In the 1970s the call for democratisation and decentralisation was especially strong in the universities. Their top-down structure was explicitly questioned when environmental activists discussed the power of experts. Scientists were asked, in effect, to step down from their ivory towers to join environmentalists, who tried to democratise environmental decision-making by distributing information among a wider public. Individual critical experts acted on behalf of environmental movements. These were the first signs of growing awareness that science is a political and democratic issue (Cramer 1989).

In 1974 the first Dutch governmental memorandum on science policy was published. Main issues or guidelines in this memorial were: that science should be guided by social needs; that quality should be controlled by selection and concentration (in 'centres of excellence'); that science should be more effective; and that organisations and structures involved in science policy be democratised. The influence of the discussions on democratisation in universities is clear from this list of issues. However, these guidelines were difficult to apply and so a discussion on steering science is still going on.

In sciences directed to environmental issues, we see the rise of thinking in terms of ecosystems and the tendency that scientists were asked to get involved in the discussions of environmental problems. As a result, possibilities for scientification of policy were created and used as well. The Scientific Council for Government Policy (WRR) was provisionally founded in 1972, and four years later was given the following responsibilities:

1. to supply on behalf of government policy scientifically sound information on developments which may affect society in the long term, to draw timely attention to anomalies and bottlenecks to be anticipated, to define major policy problems and indicate policy alternatives;
2. to provide a scientific structure which the government can use when establishing priorities and which may ensure that a consistent policy is pursued;
3. with respect to studies in the sphere of research on future developments and long-term planning in both public and private sectors, to make recommendations on the elimination of structural inadequacies, the furtherance of specific studies, and the improvement of communication and co-ordination.

In the same period, in 1973, the Dutch 'Sociaal Cultureel Planbureau' (Social Cultural Planning Office) was founded. This organisation gathers quantitative information on a wide variety of current social and cultural developments, and uses models to predict future developments to supply policy makers with a foundation on which they can formulate policy. The office was explicitly asked to contribute to the co-ordination between departments, which can be seen as derived from systemic thinking (Smits and Leyten 1991: 68).

In 1971, due to the increasing interest in environmental affairs, a new ministry was founded to cover this policy area, the 'Ministry of Public Health and Environmental Affairs' (VoMil). This department existed until 1976, when in a re-organisation Environmental Affairs moved to the new Ministry of Housing, Spatial Planning and Environmental Affairs. The first white paper on environmental policy was published in 1972. It was the reaction of the Dutch government to the degradation of the environment. The first part of this white paper stressed the importance of a systematic policy of protecting the environment and of considering the environment as an aspect in all other issues. The environmental *problematique* was understood as human interference in ecological systems. Ecological systems were seen as a set of (closely connected) sectors: air, soil, water, and organisms (including humans). A few critical environmental issues were added to these sectors: waste, radiation, and noise pollution. In the second part of the white paper priorities were set in a so-called urgency programme for every sector. Since the 'Urgentienota', the sectoral approach has been institutionalised in environmental laws and practice. The document contributed to a more broadly accepted need for a governmental environmental policy (Ast et al 1993: 179-180). The ambitions in the white paper were to repair environmental damage and to control the increasing pollution, and to define quality standards for the various sectors. The time frame for these achievements was ten years. In addition to laws, levies and information are emphasised as instruments for environmental policy in the 'Urgentienota'.

3. Economic stagnation and institutionalisation of technology policy, 1975-85

Beginning in the mid-1970s the political situation in the Netherlands sharpened. Citizens, companies and the government faced growing financial problems and social-economic stagnation (due among other things to the oil crisis). These problems were critical ones for many Western countries. While there was still a lot of public support for the environment in 1975, the attention shifted from matters of 'limits to growth' and 'quality of life' to more material topics like employment and the promotion of new technologies in the next decade.[11]

Despite the shift, the 'protest readiness' did not decline. Public involvement in general even grew. The debate on democratisation and the call for decentralisation, which had started in the early 1970s, continued. This debate started in the universities and influenced the private sector, too. An important trade union in the Netherlands, the FNV, partly changed its old centralised tendency and also became interested in company work. This can be seen as a big step towards empowering employees to influence the introduction of production technology. The problem of economic stagnation grew worse during the 1980s. Unemployment rates, already very high at the end of the 1970s, continued to increase in the early 1980s to around 15% of the working population.

---

[11] Opinion polls showed that 45.2% of the Dutch people 'agreed strongly' and a further 43.9% simply 'agreed' with the statement that the government should take severe measures to control environmental pollution. (Sociaal Cultureel Planbureau, 1978, as cited in Jamison et al., 1990, p. 152.)

Environmental problems seemed worse than ever. Whereas earlier problems were mostly restricted to air and water pollution, in the 1980s new problems emerged including soil pollution and acid rain. During the 1980s about 8,000 cases of soil pollution were discovered in the Netherlands. And in the mid-1980s new, world-wide problems came into public view, including the greenhouse problem and the depletion of the ozone layer.

Partly as a result of persistent economic stagnation and growing environmental problems, 'technology' became a magic word in the 1980s. An important question at that time was how the Netherlands would develop its economy and keep its position in the world market. Technology was seen as a promising solution to this question. The future development of industrial production became more and more important. Because of accelerating developments of new technologies in the 1980s - in particular, microelectronics, biotechnology and new materials - citizens became increasingly aware of technology (and of its impacts on society). Gradually a technology policy was developed, starting in 1979 with the first governmental white paper on technology policy, the so-called Innovatienota.

As we will see in the next section, between 1975 and 1985 the government worked steadily on policy making, expanded environmental legislation, and started developing a technology policy. The developments and experiences of this decade were an important input for environmental technology policy making in the second half of the 1980s and the first part of the 1990s.

During the second half of the 1970s nuclear energy was an important and controversial topic. While small protest actions were held in the early 1970s, not until the second half of the decade were large-scale protest actions organised. These actions varied widely. Some radical groups chained themselves to the gates of existing nuclear power stations; others constantly criticised and tried to influence the policy. The latter groups got involved in the preparation and implementation of the so-called Societal Discussion on Energy Policy ('Maatschappelijke Discussie Energiebeleid' or MDE). The government decided to organise this discussion in response to the political turmoil about the nuclear energy programme. The MDE created the possibility for all citizens to give their opinion on the future development of nuclear energy. The MDE was considered by some critics to be a failure because in the end its results did not influence policy making. Others emphasise, however, that the MDE did influence later relations between the environmental groups and the Dutch government. In this view, the MDE resulted in a more co-operative attitude on the part of the environmental movement towards the established political system, even though environmentalists kept expressing a sense of working outside the political establishment. The nuclear energy case appeared to be a catalytic factor in the politicisation of environmental groups. Their dealing with technology (and with technology policy) had to become more concrete. A critical position toward technology in general was no longer enough. To strengthen their position in the nuclear energy debate they had to give explicit opinions on technologies and to provide alternatives (Cramer 1989: 83).

4. Technology policy

In the 1980s large sums of money were spent on research in the fields of microelectronics, biotechnology and new materials. For some, 'technology' promised to solve the country's economic problems. At the same time the high unemployment rates were thought to be caused at least partly by technological developments. And unemployment was just one of the social problems the rapid technological development caused. Trade unions worked on technology agreements, in which arrangements on labour conditions were written down. Both sides of technology -- the promises concerning economic stagnation and the threats concerning employment -- made it difficult to give an opinion on technology in general. To be effective, criticism of technological developments needed to be directed explicitly to *certain* effects of technology.

During the 1970s the Dutch government was not much interested in industrial policy. Industrial policy, a responsibility of the Ministry of Economic Affairs, focused mostly on weak companies or regions. By the end of the 1970s, governmental interest in industry policy was growing. The Ministry of Science and Education produced a white paper on innovation, and two years later, in 1981, the WRR published a report on the place and future of Dutch industry. The emphasis was directed initially to a few important industries and later to a stimulation of technological developments. Governmental technology policy focused on the supply side of technological innovation.

In 1981 an advisory board on industrial policy was established, the so-called Wagner Committee. In the report of the Committee in 1981 the trend for economic policy was set for the first part of the decade: technological innovation should be heavily supported. The interest of the Ministry of Economic Affairs grew rapidly. One important consequence of this growing interest in industrial policy and technical innovation was the shift in 1982 of industrial policy making from the Ministry of Science and Education to the Ministry of Economic Affairs. The Ministry of Science kept the responsibility for the ethical and social aspects of scientific and technological developments. And in the first years after the shift, this ministry was still a driving force of technology policy.

Programmes in the emerging technology policy were directed to the most important technologies: microelectronics, biotechnology, and new materials. A first IOP, or Innovatief Onderzoek Programma, was directed to biotechnology (including agriculture and environment)[12] and has been successful with regard to new scientific outputs. Three further IOPs were directed to new materials: to Technical Ceramics (1985), Polymer Composites and Metals (1988). For information technology an unusually large programme, called Information Technology Stimulation Plan, was set up.[13] Even beyond these IOP initiatives, there were some notable measures:

- large governmental aid for some big industrial development projects, like the Megachip project (Philips and Siemens), biotechnology (Gist-Brocades N.V.) and airlines (Fokker, F-50 and F-100);
- the Programmatic Technology Stimulation directed to Companies (PBTS), to stimulate industrial R&D and applications of the three most important technologies.

Besides these three technologies, PBTS was directed to medical technology until the 1990s and since the 1990s to environmental technology. The PBTS together with the IOP are the Dutch national technology programmes.

The programmes mentioned above mostly emphasised applied research. A program directed to the developmental phase was the so-called INSTIR ('Innovatie Stimulerings Regeling', 1984-89), which compensated the labour costs of R&D in small and medium-sized companies. A credit measure specifically concentrating on the developmental phase is the 'Technology Development Credit' (TOK, Technisch Ontwikkelings Krediet). The TOK decreases the risk for companies in development

---

[12] The IOP Biotechnology ran in two cycles, during 1981-86 and during 1986-90.
[13] The ITSP ran from 1984 until 1989.

investments; only when the development project succeeds do companies have to pay back the government investment.

In general the emerging technology policy focuses on industrial technology. Little attention is paid to accompanying matters, like governmental purchases and high-risk investments. Projects that take specific societal needs as starting point, like the 'IOP Disabled People', are scarcely represented in the technology policy of the central technology policy co-ordinator, the Ministry of Economic Affairs. Such projects are located in other ministries, including those of Agriculture and Fisheries, Defence (as a customer of Dutch industry), and Transport and Water Management. As a result, technology policy is not only an emerging phenomenon but also a diffuse activity.

Although the environment was not the most important issue for the government, the ministry responsible for Environmental Affairs worked steadily on the further development of environmental policy. During the period 1975-85 environmental policy was organised by sectors; various laws were made or extended for the air, water, soil, and waste sectors. This sectoral set-up resulted in many co-ordination problems. Already by 13 June 1979 a basic law on integration of environmental regulations was adopted. This law, known as the 'Wabm'[14], was designed to increase the coherence in environmental policy and to anticipate the disadvantages of the sectoral policy and of the departmental division of the policy. Even after its adoption, this law had to be filled in for specific fields, which was time consuming.

Notwithstanding the steady development of environmental policy, the environment itself suffered continued degradation. This was regarded as being due partly to a failing government and partly to new environmental

---

[14] 'Wet algemene bepalingen milieuhygiëne'.

problems. Among the new problems were the greenhouse effect, the depletion of the ozone layer, as well as several serious cases of polluted soil and pollution of the Rhine River. Criticism of the government focused on the implementation of the policy, its sectoral approach, and the minor participation of other departments in environmental affairs. In addition, many critics asked for a more integrated approach that would be directed to *sources* of pollution, in contrast to the one-sided, often *ad hoc* attention to *effects* on the environment.

In a white paper in 1984 ('Meer dan de som der delen') the Minister of Environmental Affairs outlined a more integrated approach to the planning of environmental policy. In the same year a first 'Indicative Environmental Programme' (1985-89) was made. It introduced central themes for the next plan period of four years. This programme is a direct precursor of the present National Environmental Policy Plan (NEPP).

In 1975 the first subsidy programme to stimulate the development of "clean technology" was started. In the 1970s, thinking about the environment and technology implied thinking about what we call now 'end-of-pipe technology'. This involves technology to filter out hazardous waste before the water or air is put into the environment. An important example is the technology to clean up polluted soil. In 1979, a joint committee 'Environment and Industry' was placed in charge of the subsidy programme 'Clean Technology'. In the committee various departments are represented, as well as employer associations and one of the large technical research institutes, TNO. The committee is particularly focused on addressing bottlenecks in the development and utilisation of clean technology (Groen 1987). For example, this programme funded the development of environmental technology by companies and research institutes. The end-of-pipe approach was emphasised not only through the Clean Technology programme, but also as a result of governmental environmental policy. Since this policy was based on emission standards, companies could comply through installing (subsidised) end-of-pipe solutions.

In 1982 the first government white paper on environment and technology was jointly published by the Ministry of Economic Affairs and the Ministry of Housing and the Environment (Cramer 1996:131). The biggest part of this white paper presented an inventory of environment-protecting technologies. The white paper drew attention to the importance of environmental technology for both the development and implementation of environmental policy as well as the social-economic position of the environmental-technology-production sector. In the next two years, the second and third memorials on environmental technology were published, dealing with an 'environmental production plan'. In 1984 a group was founded to take care of the commercialisation of environmental technology know-how and its export.

5. Developing modes of technology assessment, 1986-96

Since the mid-1970s a debate developed in the Netherlands on how to assimilate technology assessment (TA) into the political system. Several proposals were put forward, stemming from discussions on microelectronics, recombinant DNA, and nuclear power. Finally, in 1984 a landmark white paper was published on *Integration of Science and Technology into Society*. The paper was positioned as a new phase of TA, where TA is linked to decision making (as was exemplified by the approach of the U.S. OTA) and is also embedded in broader political and societal processes, including the articulation of opinions and decisions about scientific and technological innovation. Accordingly, the memorandum formulated an overall goal for this new TA: broader decision making about science and technology in society. The term "broader" referred to the substantial criteria taken into account in technological development, as well as to the diversity of groups and organisations or institutions involved. The white paper argued, in effect, that the function of TA studies should be to permit societal criteria to become additional design criteria.

In the Netherlands, one result of this white paper was the establishment of two new organisations in 1986. First, the Institution for Public Information on Science and Technology (Stichting voor Publieksvoorlichting over Wetenschap en Technologie, or PWT) was founded not merely to spread information, but to stimulate awareness of the role, possibilities, shortcomings, and consequences of science and technology in the public domain. The second TA initiative was the Netherlands Organisation of Technology Assessment (NOTA), now called Rathenau Institute. NOTA's role was more focused on organising TA and making it useful for the Parliament. NOTA developed its ideas on a new and broader TA further through several projects, evaluations, and studies. In retrospect, it is possible to see two paths emerging. One path, which became dominant, focused on stimulating discussions and analysis that would contribute to social debate and to the articulation of political opinion, especially in Parliament (Rathenau Institute 1996). The Rathenau Institute used several methods for organising a broad public debate, including the Danish model of consensus conferences (cf. Andersen, ed 1995). In such a public debate a panel of citizens, recruited through advertisements in the newspapers, discusses a specific subject with experts in a well-prepared meeting lasting 2 or 3 days. The outcome is a statement made by the citizen panel containing its judgements and questions for further discussion. The experts may comment on the final statement. According to the Rathenau Institute, these debates serve a dual purpose: to introduce the viewpoints of citizens in the process of political opinion forming; and to stimulate interest in and discussion on a subject concerning society as a whole (Rathenau Institute 1994: 26).

A second path NOTA took is the development of constructive technology assessment, or CTA. A first step in NOTA's activities oriented explicitly towards CTA was a background study (Daey Ouwens et al 1987). This study was important in identifying opportunities for CTA, in highlighting the importance of what was called 'societal learning how to handle new technology,' and in offering concrete recommendations. One of the recommendations, to devote to TA studies at least 1% of the funding in every programme to stimulate technological innovation, was taken up in a few cases (the biotechnology programme being the main example). The results of this first study influenced several NOTA projects. It resulted, for example, in an emphasis on including technology developers and on articulation of design criteria in various projects. In its report *Technology Assessment: To Adjust or to Channel,* published in 1994, the section on telecommunication TA activities concluded: "this programme illustrated that it is quite feasible, and indeed pertinent, that developers of technology enter discussions with other concerned parties in society during the actual designing process and by doing so contribute towards the further development and introduction of the relevant technology" (NOTA 1994: 4).

The 1984 white paper *Integration of Science and Technology into Society* had already recognised the importance of demonstration projects in which construction principles and design criteria were developed. This approach led to a major initiative, the so-called PRISMA project, aimed at stimulating the introduction of environmentally friendly technologies in firms and other organisations (Dieleman and Hoo 1993). This project helped spread the concept of pollution prevention (as contrasted with the end-of-pipe approach) and the importance of clean technologies. Pollution prevention implies integrating environmental considerations into design processes and production.

In parallel, NOTA continued to invest in articulating the CTA perspective. In 1990, a study was done on how CTA could profit from insights from technology studies (Schot 1991). In 1991, NOTA supported (together with the Dutch Ministry of Economic Affairs) an international workshop that resulted in a book publication (Rip et al, eds 1995). In 1995, a study of CTA methodology for biotechnology firms was commissioned (Jelsma and Rip 1995). The results of these studies guide our evaluation of CTA below.

In the Netherlands, CTA was taken up by various other organisations. For example, the institute for consumer research (SWOKA) has developed a procedure called "Future Images for Consumers" for incorporating consumers and their wishes into design processes (Fonk 1994). The procedure comprises a series of meetings attended by producers and consumers, in which room is created for discussion and negotiation on design criteria by both parties. The method has been tried out in several cases, for example in a project commissioned by the Dutch Programme on Sustainable Technologies (DTO) on the introduction of novel protein foods (for replacing meat). In a final declaration, issued after a third meeting, the group stipulated design requirements for such new foods, and commented on market opportunities and possible actions (Fonk and Hamstra 1996). The DTO programme will continue to incorporate CTA elements in their activities as part of its attempt to set up so-called illustration processes of new sustainable technologies (Vergragt and van Nout 1995).

6. New directions in technology policy

At the end of the 1980s the limitations of a supply-driven technology policy were recognised. Several new initiatives were based on the need for stimulating diffusion and increasing interaction between supply and demand. The point was made that technology policies aiming at promotion and (C)TA policies are two sides of the same coin; that is, both are strategies for achieving the goals of wealth creation, sustainable development, safety and quality of life. Both aim at promoting technologies that promise to have many desirable and few undesirable impacts.

The change started with the work of the so-called Dekker Committee. The report of this committee -- with its strong emphasis on diffusion policies -- was soon labelled as the 'second phase' of technology policy. As a result, regional innovation centres were founded in 1989 to stimulate the diffusion of knowledge and technology. In addition, the Dekker Committee pleaded for a division between policy making and policy implementation, which resulted in the foundation of an agency on policy implementation, Project Stimulation Technology.

In the early 1990s, the Ministry of Economic Affairs highlighted the need for a third phase in technology policy. This phase would focus upon creating better societal embedding of new technologies and would thus complement the supply policies emphasised in the first phase and the diffusion policies of the second phase. This policy was implemented through organising strategic conferences (with a broad set of constituencies) discussing new priorities and leading to demand articulation and design criteria, and stimulating experiments with new technologies in which citizens participate. An example of the latter is Digital City Amsterdam, a project in which citizens experiment with e-mail and Internet, build user competence, and provide input for further technology development. A series of educational initiatives also forms part of the policy.

With the issuing of the landmark report *Our Common Future* by the World Commission on Environment and Development in 1987, the drive for "sustainable development" became a central issue in Dutch environmental policies. The concept of sustainable development worked as a mobilising concept for deeper and more fundamental changes. This message was reinforced by the publication in 1988 of *Zorgen voor Morgen* (Concerns for Tomorrow) by the National Institute of Public Health and Environmental Protection (RIVM). This report argued that the environment was in an alarming state and called for reducing the release of pollutants by between 70% and 90% and halving energy consumption. Already this report earmarked the development and diffusion of environmental technology to play an important role.

The challenges posed by both these reports were taken up in the *National Environmental Policy Plan* of 1989 (NEPP). The Ministry of Housing, Spatial Planning and Environment (VROM) had an important role in initiating the preparation of the NEPP, working together with three other ministries (Economic Affairs; Agriculture, Nature Management and Fisheries; and Transport, Public Works and Water Management). The concept of sustainable development was incorporated into Dutch policy in terms of three objectives:

1. Closing substance cycles in the chain of raw materials, production process, product, waste and associated emissions;
2. Saving energy along with increasing efficiency and using renewable energy sources;
3. Improving quality (above quantity) of products, production processes, raw materials, waste, and the environment to extend the use of substances in the economic cycle.

From these objectives, the cornerstone of sustainability can be derived: effectively controlling the entire life cycle of products from raw materials to wastes. The need to manage the waste chain as a whole (the so-called cradle-to-grave approach) calls for government policies and business strategies extending over the whole life cycle of a product.

The NEPP created a new set of objectives and provided a sense of urgency in dealing with environmental problems, now captured in the idea of sustainable development. In terms of concrete policies, we would like to discuss two concrete avenues of changes. First, the NEPP reinforced a set of new policies which led to more consultation between government and industry. Second, it created space for new initiatives to stimulate environmental technology. The call for shared responsibility in the NEPP resulted in voluntary agreements. Such agreements, or covenants, are written down but have no formal judicial or legal status. The idea is that the private sector will agree to and commit to these agreements more readily or more quickly, because their opinions and possibilities have been taken into account. Another reason to use this instrument is the existence of the European Union's competition laws, which do not easily accept country-specific product rules (owing to a concern that they might distort competition). However, it is hard to tell whether voluntary agreements are a successful instrument, because no systematic evaluation has been made of their effectiveness in meeting environmental goals as compared to more-traditional command-and-control regulation. A general observation is that the more widely varied the target groups are, the more difficult it is to come to agreements.

In a research paper on "Joint environmental policy-making in comparative perspective," voluntary agreements are called examples of the more general concept of joint environmental policy-making (Mol 1996). Joint environmental policy-making is defined as "new environmental policy initiatives that have as a common denominator more co-operative, participative and interactive ways of environmental policy formation and implementation aimed at consensus building of goals, strategies and implementation time paths." Joint environmental policy instruments are put forward as alternatives to traditional command-and-control regulation, promising to turn the tide of state failure.

Another relatively new instrument in environmental policy which created opportunities for public involvement in technological choices is the Environmental Impact Assessment (Milieu Effect Rapportage or MER). Since 1987 an EIA is required for significant extensions of facilities or plants. It is a framework or methodology specifically developed to minimise the potential environmental impacts of new developments at the earliest stage possible: the design and development stage. The EIA system aims at taking the environment fully into account in decision-making. According to the present experiences, it works well as an instrument of gathering extra environmental data. The question is whether this information is taken into account, resulting in more environmentally sound decisions. The simple fact is that many other factors influence the final decision as well. The EIA procedure is open to public: individuals or interest groups can react to already-gathered information, or introduce alternative information.

7. Conclusions: an emerging environmental technology policy

By the end of the 1980s the tide was turning for environmental technology, as Cramer (1996) points out. As in technology policy generally, in the field of environmental technology more attention is being paid to the diffusion of knowledge and technology and to the integration of supply and demand. In 1988 the National Environment Centre, an initiative of the private sector, was founded. The centre functions as bridge between the supply and demand sides of environmental technology. Besides the innovation centres mentioned above, Innovation Centres for Environmental Services are founded to help medium and small companies in applying environmental technology. Two new, demand-driven initiatives are the technology programmes known as DTO and EET.

The Sustainable Technology Development Programme (DTO)

An example of the more integrated and long-term environmental technology policy is the Sustainable Technology Development programme. The Ministry of Housing, Spatial Planning and Environment (VROM) now works in close co-operation with four other ministries: the Ministries of Agriculture, Nature Protection and Fisheries; of Transport, Public Works and Water Management; of Economic Affairs; and of Education and Science. Three elements were considered to be of critical importance if such a programme was to have any hope of success (DTO 1994).

First, the specific challenges to technology that were embodied in the term 'sustainability' had to be defined and quantified to the fullest extent possible. When asked for advice, the Council for Environment and Nature Research (RMNO) identified two parallel approaches: sustainability implies a more equitable access to global resources among the world's population; sustainability also implies that environment, development, and peace are inseparable, and that future generations have the same rights to environmental resources. Second, a methodology had to be developed for addressing these challenges. In order to facilitate a process that enables the fundamental changes accompanying sustainable technologies, a 'backcasting' approach was adopted. With backcasting one first tries to conceptualise, describe, and quantify as many concrete elements as possible of a desired future objective. One next traces a route back from that future to the present. Research and development then may be tuned to this long-term situation and directed along this route. The time horizon is about 30 years; the method typically assumes that environmental impacts should be reduced to one-twentieth of their present levels in order to meet the long-term 'eco-capacity'. In 'illustration processes' the desired technological development is defined, which results in a 'manual for research and development' that can direct the concerned parties towards sustainability. And third, since sustainability is clearly an international, if not global, concern, an international network had to be established for exchange of information, collaborative research, and dissemination of findings in similar or related fields.

Economy, Ecology and Technology (EET)

In a 1995 governmental white paper 'Kennis in beweging' ('Knowledge in motion') it is noted that tensions exist between economic growth and ecological sustainability. As a result the ministries of Economic Affairs and of Science, Culture and Education started a new subsidy programme called Economy, Ecology and Technology. In this programme attention is directed to prevention and process-integrated technology. The program aims at co-operation between research institutes and companies, to create technological 'breakthroughs' in 5 to 20 years. These 'breakthroughs' should bridge the gap between economy and ecology, promising to be commercial in the future, too. Proposals of co-operative projects must fit in at least one of the six themes of the programme (EET 1995):

1. Substantial decrease of environmental degradation caused by process water, including cooling water, in Dutch industry;
2. Substantial decrease of the waste problem in Dutch industry;
3. Complete integration of the environment in the product-development process;
4. Substantial limiting of emissions and energy use in traffic and transport;
5. Substantial use of renewable resources;
6. Substantial use of renewable sources of energy.

Subsidies are given for the following stages of development: fundamental research, industrial research, and pre-competitive development. The 1996 budget is Hfl 20 billion, increasing to 45 billion a year. These programs indicate that an environmental technology policy is developing in the Netherlands, in many ways in a more ambitious manner than in any other country in Europe.

References

Andersen, I.E. (ed.) (1995) *Feasibility Study on New Awareness Initiatives,* Danish Board of Technology, Copenhagen

Arentsen, M.J., J.Th.A. Bressers, P-J. Klok (1993) *Twintig jaar milieubeleid: van Urgentienota en verder*

Ast, Mr. J.A. van, Drs. H. Geerlings (1993) `Milieukunde & Milieubeleid - een introductie',* Samson H.D. Tjeenk Willink, Alphen aan den Rijn

Cramer, J (1989) *De groene golf - geschiedenis en toekomst van de milieubeweging,* Jan van Arkel, Utrecht

Cramer, J (1996) `Veranderingen binnen het milieutechnologiebeleid' in: `Leren met beleid - beleidsverandering en beleidsgericht leren bij nimby-, milieu- en technologiebeleid',* Eberg, Jan, Rinie van Est & Henk van de Graaf (ed.) Het Spinhuis

Daey Ouwens, C., P. van Hoogstraten, J. Jelsma, F. Prakke and A. Rip, *Constructief Technologisch Aspectenonderzoek. Een verkenning,* Den Haag: staatsuitgeverij, 1987. (NOTA, voorstudie 4).

Dieleman, H. and S. de Hoo (1993) "Understanding Technological Responses of Industrial Firms to Environmental Problems: Implications for Government Policy,"in *Environmental Strategies for Industry,* K. Fischer and Johan Schot, eds., Island Press, Washington, D.C.

DTO (1994) `Looking back from the future', Dutch governmental programme for Sustainable Technology Development,* Editor: Programmabureau Interdepartementaal Onderzoekprogramma DTO

EET (1995) `Economie, Ecologie en Technologie - Meerjarige ondersteuning van duurzame technologische ontwikkelingen',* brochure.

Fonk, G.J. (1994) *Een constructieve rol van de consument in technologie-ontwikkeling. Constructief Technologisch Aspectenonderzoek vauit consumentenoptiek,* SWOKA, The Hague, Ph.D. thesis, University of Twente

Fonk, G.J. and Hamstra, A. (1996) *Toekomstbeelden voor consumenten van Novel Protein Foods,* Delft, Programma DTO, werkdocument VN12

Groen, M., B. Scholtens, J. van Kasteren (1987) `Milieutechnologie - Meer dan milieu en technologie',* Staatsuitgeverij, 's-Gravenhage

Innovatienota - Het overheidsbeleid inzake technologische vernieuwing in de Nederlandse samenleving, Tweede Kamer, zitting 1979-1980, 15 855, nrs. 1-2.

Jamison, A., R. Eyerman and J. Cramer (1990) *The Making of the New Environmental Consciousness - A Comparative Study of the Environmntal Movements in Sweden, Denmark and the Netherlands,* Edinburgh Univerity Press

Jelsma, J. and Rip, A., with a contribution y J.L. van os (1995) *Biotechnologie in Bedrijf. Een bijdrage van Constructief Technology Assessment aan biotechnologisch innoveren,* The Hague: Rathenau Institute

Ministerie van Economische Zaken (1995) *Kennis in beweging,* Den Haag

Ministerie van Onderwijs en Wetenschappen, *Integratie van Wetenschap en Technologie in de samenleving. Beleidsnota,* 's-Gravenhage: Tweede Kamer 1983-1984, 18 421, nrs. 1-2.

Mol, Artur, P.J., Volkmar Lauber, Martin Enevoldsen and Jolle Landman (1996) "Joint environmental policy-making in comparative perspective", presented at the Greening of Industry Network conference, Heidelberg, Germany.

NOTA (1996) *Technology Assessment: To Adjust or to Channel,* Den Haag

Rathenau Institute (1994) *The Rathenau Institute and the debate, Annual report 1994,* Den Haag

Rathenau Instituut (1996) *Van technologisch aspectenonderzoek tot maatschappelijk debat, 10 jaar NOTA-Rathenau Instituut 1986-1996,* Den Haag

Rip, A., T.J. Misa and J. Schot (eds) (1995) *Managing Technology in Society - The Approach of Constructive Technology Assessment,* Pinter, London

Schot, J.W. (1991) Technology Dynamics: An Inventory of Policy Implications for Constructive Technology Assessment, in: *Maatschappelijke Sturing van Technische Ontwikkeling. Constructief Technology Assessment als hedendaags Luddisme,* Ph.D. thesis, Universiteit Twente, Enschede

Smits, R. and J. Leyten (1991) *Technology Assessment: waakhond of speurhond?,* Dissertation University of Amsterdam, Kerkebosch bv, Zeist

Vergragt, Ph., and D. van Nout (1995) "Introducing the mobile hydrogen fuel cell", paper presented at the Fourth Greening of Industry Network conference, Toronto

WRR (1991) *Verschuivingen in het technologiebeleid - Een internationale vergelijking vanuit de praktijk,* Voorstudies en achtergronden Technologiebeleid, T6, Roobeek, J.M. en E. Broesterhuizen, SDU, Den Haag

The British National Experience

by Patrick van Zwanenberg[*]

1. Introduction

It is difficult to conceive of British environmental science and technology policy as anything more than the sum of diverse clusters of activities scattered throughout different policy sectors. Most policy activities have been managed on a departmental or agency level, historically with little overall coordination, and to some extent that situation still remains, both for the 'policy for science' dimensions of supporting and directing environmentally-related research and the 'science for policy' interests in regulatory and administrative matters. A further distinctive feature of this area of British policy is that direct government involvement in the development of environmental technology barely exists, even though this is a central feature of environmental science and technology policy in many other countries.

Two leading analysts of British policy-making have argued that "[w]e see it as a matter of fact that most political activity [in the UK] is bargained in private worlds by special interests and interested specialists." (Jordan and Richardson 1987, p. ix); a characterisation that is no less apt for environmental science and technology policy-making processes as it is for

---

[*] My thanks to Robin Grove-White, Brian Wynne and other colleagues at the Centre for the Study of Environmental Change, Lancaster University for their advice and helpful comments.

UK policy-making in general. Indeed, policy, for the most part, has been made by shifting combinations of state authorities and representatives drawn from the industrial sector in alliance with small but extremely important groups of scientific and technical experts drawn from both academia and industry. There has been only relatively limited scope for formal participation by environmental groups or other organised civic interests in environmental science and technology policy as a whole, and almost none whatsoever with regard to the management and promotion of research and development. The policy-making process is also particularly opaque in Britain - a characteristic supported by explicit and legally sanctioned principles of official secrecy - which throws up additional barriers to public participation. Nevertheless, Britain has an extremely vibrant and diverse environmental movement and the civic domain has played an important role in the environmental science and technology field, developing counter-expertise and utilising those political opportunity structures that do exist to influence both policy and wider political sensibilities, whether through formal or informal means or via mechanisms that bypass the state altogether.

The diversity of the British environmental movement makes it difficult to generalise about the political strategy or the status of various groups in the policy process. Nevertheless, during the 1970s and 1980s, whilst environmental science and technology policy remained fragmented and decentralised with government, particularly during the 1980s, taking an obstructive stance towards environmental progress, much of the environmental movement operated largely outside of central policy-making communities. Attention was directed at those administrative structures that allowed at least some form of participation, for example, public inquiries, Parliamentary Select Committees and Royal Commissions. General lobbying and campaigning activities were targeted at both government and industry and conflicts between Britain and the European Union were productively exploited in both the policy and wider political domains. Since 1988 the British government belatedly began a process of integrating environmental priorities into other government policies and the traditional closed and fragmented nature of environmental science and technology policy began to shift somewhat towards a more centralised, formal approach. A diverse range of strategies continue to be used by environmental groups, including direct consultation with industry, and attempts to influence both consumer and financial markets and private innovation processes. In the 1990s, some moderate sections of the environmental movement appear to be becoming far more legitimate and permanent actors in central policy-making processes. At the same time, however, wider programmes of state disengagement from economic and administrative concerns and the general growth of market cultures have meant that many facets of environmental science and technology policy are increasingly becoming the responsibility of, or are primarily orientated towards, the private sector. One consequence is that public participation in a general sense is being shifted from a politically articulated mode (albeit a relatively limited one) to the idea of agency through individual consumption in the marketplace.

The development of environmental science and technology policy in the UK can be construed, at least in part, as a product of the interplay between bureaucratic, economic, academic and civic 'policy cultures' (Elzinga and Jamison 1995) This chapter provides a preliminary account of the evolution of this area of policy with reference to the different roles of those four policy cultures in shaping and reformulating environmental institutions, policy agendas and discourse. The chapter begins by outlining some pertinent features of UK political and policy-making culture, features which have themselves been affected by other factors such as globalisation, the European Union and the growth of market cultures. We then provide an historical account, from the early 1970s to date, of the development and reconstitution of environmental science and technology policy in the UK. We focus on the main areas, opportunities for, and experiences of public engagement in this arena, describing how these have changed through the 1980s and into the very different context of the 1990s.

2. Environmental Science and Technology Policy-Making Styles

British environmental science and technology policy-making 'styles' are shaped in important ways by the particular roles that scientists and other experts play in the policy-making process, especially when considered in relation to the dominant approach to decision-making - a process of 'bureaucratic accommodation' in which closed and privileged 'policy communities' negotiate decisions in ways that attempt to avoid electoral politics and public conflict. (Jordan & Richardson 1982)

The mobilization of scientists and technicians by the British government during the second world war cemented what up to that point had been a slowly growing alliance between scientists and the bureaucracy. Senior academic scientists like Henry Tizard who had chaired the Scientific Advisory Committee to the War Cabinet became chair of the Advisory Committee on Scientific Policy, set up in 1947 to advise on the execution of civil scientific policy. (Vig 1968) In the post-war period elite groups of academic and industrial scientists have been invited to become involved in an extensive system of expert advisory committees, royal commissions and committees of inquiry. They have also become members of research councils and other quasi government organisations involved in scientific aspects of policy, and have acted on secondment as departmental chief scientists. The criteria for appointment are opaque but the scientists are generally eminent, and share similar educational backgrounds. (Ince 1986; Gummett 1980) Expert advisory groups rarely include representatives of public interest groups whereas industry scientists are routinely included.

Advisory committees have close and informal ties with government activities in environmental science and technology, and officials tend to defer, or at least portray themselves as deferring, to expert committees of scientists in many areas of policy. As with so many aspects of British policy-making, it is difficult to study how policy decisions are actually reached in the environmental science and technology domain; the types of negotiations and conflicts that occur both within expert committees and between scientists and other actors in the policy-making process are usually not amenable to public scrutiny. As with the rest of central government, expert committees lack transparency and clear accountability, proceedings are not published and the committees are not generally subject to requirements of due process. It is clear, however, that expert committees play an important role as consensus building mechanisms and in providing legitimacy to policy, as well as in the provision of policy-relevant advice. (Everest 1990) These different roles can be clearly appreciated in relation to more general aspects of British policy-making.

For many dimensions of British policy, decision-making occurs and is sustained predominantly within what political scientists have termed 'policy communities'. These tend to be organised around individual government departments and their client groups - usually producer interests - and membership is usually restricted to interests that share common policy predispositions, preferred technological trajectories, and similar definitions of what is considered relevant and accepted knowledge. (Rhodes 1988; Laffin 1986) Policy communities are relatively insulated from other government departments, the general public and Parliament and official secrecy helps to maintain an opaque system of decision-making.

Participation in policy communities is usually confined to whatever minimum number of interests must be informed in order to operationalise policy with the object being to get as wide agreement as possible among those participants. (Jordan & Richardson 1982; Council for Science and Society 1982) A general tradition of pragmatism in British policy culture is reflected within environmental policy domains in an emphasis on the practical workability of policy. That is, a sensitivity to both economic and practical constraints on corporate activity and a concern that regulations are technically effective and flexible enough to accommodate situational variability. (Lowe & Flynn 1989; O'Riordan & Weale 1989) Thus within environmental science and technology domains, a trusted and closed network of scientific and policy actors can resolve and negotiate technical and social conflicts without engendering wider public and political conflict. It is important to note that this system of 'bureaucratic accommodation' is restricted to the privileged and restricted set of actors within a policy community. Once in the wider political domain, policy-making is generally represented as non-deliberative and entirely unambiguous.

This closed, unaccountable policy style, negotiable within the policy community and non-deliberative outside it, is rooted in a more general political culture around government in which the appointed institutions operate in a highly discretionary and paternalistic fashion. (Wynne *et al* 1996) In turn, that culture reflects the general system of British governance, especially its highly centralised and powerful executive and the relatively limited mechanisms of executive accountability - features that have deeper roots in the constitutional basis of government in Britain. (Hutton 1995) In terms of the four policy cultures we can conceive of environmental science and technology policy-making involving actors within the bureaucratic and economic domains, with elite representatives of the academic domain. Representatives drawn from the civic policy domain may occasionally be included in some realms of policy, especially if they possess relevant expertise or are crucial to policy implementation.

A further distinctive feature of British environmental science and technology policy, at least in terms of our interest with public engagement, concerns the ways in which most official framings of 'environmental problems' have been highly reductionist in nature and the relevant knowledges defined extremely narrowly. A culture of 'sound science' is deeply entrenched in UK institutional arrangements and partly because of the pre-eminent status of physics in British advisory bodies since the second world war, the notion of 'sound science' tends to be dominated by physicist paradigms of precise and controlled forms of knowledge. (Wynne *et al* 1996) Most environmental issues and related research agendas have been framed accordingly, and consequently, there is a tendency, across a wide variety of environmentally-related sectors, to adopt a highly conservative approach to policy in the absence of particular conceptions of 'scientific proof' of environmental damage. Although not necessarily unique to the UK, these framing assumptions have remained relatively impermeable to challenge within official fora, due largely to particularities of the British polity.

Indeed, this scientistic culture intersects in quite problematic ways with other features of the policy-making process. For example, pragmatic concerns that regulations should be able to accommodate situational variability and that decision-making procedures should have room for tacit expert judgment are reflected in a reluctance to adopt explicit quantified or codified strategies for conducting risk assessments and other aspects of science-based policy. (Wynne *et al* 1996) Moreover, the scientistic and non-deliberative portrayal of decision-making underpins a tendency not to examine, and a determination not to be challenged on, particular science-based decisions. All this poses obvious problems for critical actors who wish to question dominant approaches to scientific assessment and attempt to broaden the horizon of possible policy responses.

More generally, participation by actors located in the civic domain is hampered by an absence of alternative routes of dissent. Parliament and the judiciary have relatively weak powers of oversight; the British electoral system has prevented green parties from achieving representation, and there is a general absence of other constitutional checks and balances. Furthermore, local and regional government is extremely weak and does not provide a particularly useful point of influence. As a consequence virtually the only way that environmental groups have been able to engage *formally* with the policy process is by being accepted as members of the various policy communities. Access, however, is entirely by discretion and custom and unwritten codes of sensible and moderate behaviour have meant that environmental groups wishing to participate in formal policy processes are required to adopt relatively moderate positions, seeking policy as opposed to structural change. (Lowe and Goyder 1983)

Despite this picture of a closed, narrowly scientistic environmental science and technology policy-making style, it is important to note that policy-making processes inevitably vary between different arenas and issues and they are not necessarily static within any one area of policy. Some aspects of policy-making might be better characterised as 'issue networks' insofar as they contain larger number of competing interests operating in a less stable and interdependent way than policy communities. (Laffin 1986) In addition, formerly closed and stable policy communities may present internal conflicts when new political or commercial contingencies entail adjustments to groups preferred policy predispositions. Processes of deregulation and privatisation and, in particular, the growing influence of the European Union, have sometimes destabilised, often quite substantially, the interests involved in, and priorities adopted within existing policy communities. (*cf* Smith 1989) These types of structural fractures and dynamic processes may well create, close down and/or alter the nature of different types of political opportunity structures and consequently the extent and ways in which previously excluded environmental groups and the public can and do engage in science and technology policy issues.

3. Phases in the Development of UK Environmental Science and Technology Policy

Environmental concern in the UK is a long-standing phenomena. During the late nineteenth century a number of organisations essentially concerned with preservation such as the National Trust and the Garden Cities Association (now the Town and Country Planning Association) were established as part of a late Victorian reaction, primarily amongst relatively elite sections of the population, to the consequences of urban industrialisation and some of the tenets of economic liberalism. During the inter-war years, the social-base of mainstream environmental concern widened to include elements of the suburban middle-class in concerns about government regulation, especially in relation to land-use planning and pollution control. Groups such as the Council for the Preservation of Rural England and a number of local organisations concerned with amenity were established. Many of the post-war controls on development, national parks and green belts emerged from this movement. (Newby 1990) There is also a tradition of more militant environmental groups emerging during this period that drew on a broader social constituency. The Commons Preservation Society (established in 1865), for example, sought both lawful and unlawful means to prevent the increasing transformation of common land into exclusive private ownership. Similarly, during the inter-war period, industrial workers from Manchester and Sheffield organised demonstrations and mass trespasses in an attempt to reopen access to the countryside in the Peak District which was being fenced off to protect grouse-breeding. (Rüdig 1995)

In the post-war period there has been a sustained growth of the environment as a central dimension of public debate. Air pollution, nature conservation and the health and environmental consequences of radioactive fallout from atmospheric weapons testing, for example, were issues of emerging public concern and policy response in the 1950s. In the 1960s, however, 'the environment' emerged as an area of key political importance in the UK.

3.1 The 1960s and early 1970s - Institutional Innovation

Although the earlier mainstream environmental concerns with preservation and regulation remained, many of the escalating public anxieties in the 1960s were concerned with broader conceptions of social well-being. In particular, environmental concerns were a response to what was perceived as an increasing and collectively uncontrolled technological, corporate and bureaucratic regulation of social life, an opposition to excessive materialism, and a lack of confidence in the beneficial effects of science and technology. These concerns were crystallised by incidents such as the *Torrey Canyon* oil pollution crisis in the English Channel in 1967, as well events overseas such as the publication of Carson's *Silent Spring* in 1962 and the mercury poisoning incident in Minamata Bay.

As discussed above, a significant section of the UK environmental movement, at least in terms of membership, predates the public concerns of the late 1960s and early 1970s. Nevertheless large numbers of dynamic local groups were established during this period as well as national campaigning groups such as Friends of the Earth, Transport 2000 and Greenpeace which helped to revitalise and refocus the older more established groups. The newer more radical groups tended to focus far more on the wider social conditions and practices that gave rise to environmental damage as opposed to the older groups' traditional concerns with preserving traditional habitat and green-field sites and limiting the expansion of industrial development.

A range of institutional reforms and policy responses accompanied the upswell of public concern. For example, in 1967 the Natural Environment Research Council was established and in 1970 the first White Paper on the environment was published. In the same year a Royal Commission on Environmental Pollution, a body comprised of scientists and prominent public figures with a remit to produce an annual review of important pollution issues, was created. Also in 1970 the Department of the Environment (DoE) was established, combining housing policy, local government, transport and a new pollution unit. In 1974 the Control of Pollution Act (an early consequence of EU membership) was also enacted as a first attempt to establish a comprehensive environmental protection framework. Nevertheless, many key aspects of environmental science and technology policy were still implemented at local level, and split amongst different government departments. Recognising this fragmentation, the new Royal Commission on Environmental Pollution (RCEP) recommended in 1976 that regulation of discharges to air, water and land should no longer be administered by different central, regional and local agencies and should instead be integrated under one unified central inspectorate. This advice on policy reform was ignored by government until the late 1980s. (O'Riordan & Weale 1989)

On the whole, environmental issues were responded to by government in the early 1970s primarily as technical and administrative problems - to be managed by experts largely within existing and reformed institutional structures. The gap between this official response and wider public concerns about the social, political and cultural conditions underpinning environmental problems created tensions which regularly surfaced in subsequent years. (Grove-White 1991)

3.2 Protest, Policy and Public Inquiries in the 1970s

Environmental politics in the 1970s were dominated by a series of issues - relating in particular to transport infrastructure, minerals extraction and nuclear power - that found public expression through the British land-use planning system. As one of the few policy fora that allowed certain forms of public participation, land-use planning, and in particular the public inquiry system, provided political opportunity structures which the environmental movement gravitated towards and in the process helped to frame the domestic environmental agenda of the 1970s.

All development in the UK, excluding agriculture and forestry, is subject to the permission of local planning authorities. For large planning proposals that are either rejected by the local authority or for which, at the relevant Ministers discretion, there are deemed to be objections of substance and national interest (for example, because a power station is of a new design) a public inquiry is held. Such inquiries take the form of tribunals at which evidence for and against a proposal may be given. Inquiries have relatively restricted powers and are essentially advisory mechanisms. They are officially supposed to aid implementation of pre-existing policy created elsewhere in democratic institutions (i.e. Parliament). Under Ministerial terms of reference, inquiries, led by an appointed Inspector, consider objections from local interests (for example property-holders) affected by the specific development. The intention is to inform Ministers about the *local application* of policy.

Thus the inquiry process involves an underlying presumption in favour of development with the wider policy framework exempt from questioning by objectors on the grounds that these are issues for which Ministers are directly answerable to Parliament and are consequently inappropriate for consideration at local inquiries. During the 1970s objectors to major public inquiries, for example, into nuclear power stations and roads, discovered that government were reluctant to actually articulate explicit policies on, for example, energy production or transport strategy. Furthermore, objectors identified a failure on the part of Parliament and the Executive to control or oversee policy. In the civil nuclear power community, for example, shared political concerns about energy dependency, psychological links between nationalism and the development of nuclear power and the military roots of the civil nuclear programme underpinned a commitment to expanding nuclear power. The technocratic basis of nuclear policy was bolstered by extreme secrecy and a virtually unquestioned legitimacy of scientists at the Atomic Energy Association (AEA). Parliament and even Ministers effectively deferred a series of policy questions to the AEA and as a consequence a range of safety, cost and need issues were effectively kept off the policy agenda or if such issues did arise, they were safely contained within the policy community. (Saward 1992)

Moreover objectors identified an increasing tendency to naturalise political commitments into a language of technical 'facts', for example in relation to energy demand growth and traffic forecasting. Objectors thus approached inquiries as a means of engaging with inaccessible institutions and exposing this spurious technicisation of politics, especially since Parliament was evidently failing to scrutinise what was in effect the production of policy by private interests. When policy examination by objectors was refused on the grounds that Parliamentary democracy should not be undermined by self-selected private interests, environmental groups directly challenged the policy framework, especially at road infrastructure inquiries, in the form of well-publicised sit-ins and disruptions. (Levin 1979)

The public inquiry system has developed *ad hoc* from initiatives taken during the nineteenth century enclosure movement whereby Parliament delegated some of its responsibilities over settling land ownership rights to the Executive. Because the scope of planning lacked clarity from the relevant legislation the inquiry system was highly elastic and its terms of reference can easily be enlarged or closed in response to external political pressures. Novel arguments by objectors concerning aspects of 'policy' that ought to be contestable in public inquiries were often accommodated by inspectors. For example, at the 1977 Windscale nuclear inquiry into the THORP reprocessing plant the terms of reference were enlarged *ad hoc* as a result of intense public pressure and allowed environmental groups to question official institutions' evaluations of nuclear risks, costs and need. (Wynne 1982) . Yet even though, in this case, the policy framework was allowed to be partially addressed, government officials were not allowed to be cross-examined. Moreover, although inspectors could accommodate demands for policy examination there was no guarantee that any account would be taken of such criticisms in the final decision and participants at Windscale later criticised the inquiry as being only a charade of apparent public participation. Whilst elastic terms of reference allowed environmental objectors to pursue progressively more strategic arguments during the discussion of individual developments the inquiry system has also proved to be effective at containing environmental tensions within the discipline of the inquiry framework, especially in relation to other institutional procedures for processing environmental demands.

Environmental groups and other objectors were well aware that public inquiries served as exercises in public relations but although planning decisions were rarely settled in favour of objectors they did provide highly visible entry points for public argument and for arousing the attention of both the media and the public. Moreover, through their experience of public inquiries, many environmental groups developed important sources of counter-expertise and began a process of slowly exposing the flimsy basis upon which arguments were made, for example, over the cost and safety of nuclear energy; in this case, arguments that were later exonerated once the attempt to privatise the nuclear industry was made in the late 1980s.

The planning system was not the only focus for environmental tensions or attempts at public technology assessment, but merely the most visible and successful route through which certain 'environmental' issues reached the political agenda in the UK.

Organisations such as Social Audit in the early 1970s, the Council for Science and Society in the late 1970s and the British Society for Social Responsibility in Science sought to provide a role for public assessment of technology and the provision of research for trade unions and other public interest and environmental groups. Various initiatives by trades unions, the most well known of which occurred at Lucas Aerospace, sought to propose diversification in technological production. The Lucas Joint Shop Stewards' Alternative Corporate Plan identified what were argued to be socially useful and environmentally appropriate products and production methods that could be switched to as a result of the Labour government's defence cuts. These plans met considerable resistance from management, not over the technical or marketing details but because of the challenge to management prerogative. Some environmental groups, for example the Socialist Environment Resources Association were also successful in committing some of the trades unions and the Labour Party to anti-nuclear policies in the late 1970s.

Yet, in general, most forms of public engagement were only operating at a very late stage of decision-making in the policy-making process or were only taking place in the wider political domain. There was little immediate effect on policy itself or the way policy processes operated. For example, energy research and development priorities continued to be strongly biased towards nuclear power with very little support for renewables, combined heat and power or energy efficiency. (Wynne & Crouch 1991)

At the same time, the economic recession following the 1973/4 oil price hike prevented much progress in UK environmental policy. Many of the clauses of the 1974 Control of Pollution Act were simply not enacted because public expenditure constraints prevented capital investment in, for example, waste treatment facilities. Private investment in pollution control equipment and in replacing obsolete plant also slowed markedly. Similarly public environmental R&D declined by about 25% in the late 1970s. (Wynne & Crouch 1991) Improvements in air and water pollution did occur, however, but were primarily a consequence of the sharp contraction in manufacturing industry.

3.3 Neo-Liberalism: 1979-1988

At the beginning of the decade, environmental concerns faced not only an adverse economic climate but also a government wholly antagonistic to environmental protection. Leaked Cabinet papers, for example, recorded the intention of the 1979 administration to 'reduce over-sensitivity to environmental considerations' (*Sunday Times,* 18th November 1979) Indeed from 1979 to 1988 there were relatively few initiatives of domestic origin in public policy that improved environmental protection (notably, the end of sea disposal of nuclear waste) Yet a whole slew of environmental issues ranging from food safety, water and marine pollution and nuclear waste disposal to transboundary air pollution, ozone depletion and global climate change dominated environmental politics in the 1980s. Several reasons underpinned this increasing politicisation of the environment: government hostility to and neglect of environmental problems which made for numerous potential targets for the environmental movement; the growing sophistication and lobbying expertise of environmental groups as well as a growing technical counter-expertise; conflicts between the UK government and the EU and other Member States which pushed issues into the public domain and provided useful points of leverage for environmental groups; growing middle-class resentment in the south of the country (which experienced an economic boom in the mid to late 1980s) at neglected public infrastructure; and finally, a tendency for 'the environment' to provide a focus for collective social concerns at a time when dominant public discourse focused on market individualism. (Grove-White 1991)

The neo-liberal agenda introduced under the 1979 Thatcher administration involved a general rolling back of the State in economic and administrative matters and the political resurgence of business interests. This was reflected in trends towards deregulation and the promotion of market mechanisms in preference to administrative controls, a programme of privatising publicly owned industries, and a general move to reduce costs to and burdens on British industry. These trends had a number of important consequences for British environmental science and technology policy.

Firstly, deregulation was explicitly pursued on the planning system. Through, for example, the repeal of the Community Land Act in 1980 the introduction of 'enterprise zones' and 'simplified planning zones' and the use of 'Special Development Orders', the government sought to free-up the land and property market from development controls and shift decision-making powers away from local authorities and local democratic processes to private developers and agencies of central government (Blowers 1987). Impediments to large developments were also eased. For example a Special Development Order was used to exempt exploratory investigation of potential sites for the disposal of low-level nuclear waste from public inquiries. Similarly, there were no public inquiries for the Channel Tunnel and a major bridge across the Thames in east London. (Blowers 1987; Whitelegg 1989)

As one of the few types of environmental regulation that was at least in part accountable to local democratic procedures, the planning system was less attuned to business interests that other areas of environmental policy, and thus an obvious target for deregulation. Furthermore, the Conservative Party's close links to construction interests (who were actively campaigning against the costs and difficulties associated with the planning system) and the government's concerted effort to decimate local government autonomy added to the administration's deregulatory zeal. Other environmental policy arenas were also weakened although less explicitly. Thus pressures to minimise financial burdens on industry were exerted on regulatory agencies, there were cuts in regulatory agencies' budgets and staff, and a shift to greater representation of business interests on agencies' governing councils and advisory boards. (Lowe & Flynn 1989)

Secondly, the government's reluctance to impose any additional financial burdens of British industry coincided conveniently with the cultural tendency within the science policy community to demand scientifically definitive proof of harm prior to changing policy. In the case of transboundary air pollution (i.e. acid rain) and North sea pollution, for example, the government adopted a cautious stance despite considerable international pressure. Moreover the government initially attempted to slow down the movement towards the Montreal Protocol on CFCs and failed to implement, and/or challenged a number of EU Directives relating to the environment.

More generally, the tendency to frame risk and environmental issues in a highly reductionist way underpinned public controversy in a range of policy areas. For example, in the area of pesticide regulation, the regulatory regime is primarily concerned with sanctioning commercial claims about pesticide efficacy and managing health and environmental risks. Broader risk issues about, for example, the need for agrochemicals, the magnitude of use, and the general nature of UK agricultural strategy are excluded from the regulatory regime's remit. Furthermore, pesticide regulation is typically construed, at least by government, entirely as a technical and administrative matter, and the presence of an expert advisory committee comprised of independent scientists (in the sense that they are not directly employed by government or private industry) is considered to represent the public interest. Extensive secrecy prevented public knowledge of procedure, decision-making within the regime, and underlying rationales. Administrative arrangements also ensured that less direct public participation, for example, via judicial and parliamentary oversight were also strictly limited. This was achieved, for example, not only be an opaque regulatory system but also by establishing and maintaining the regime within a non-statutory administrative framework until 1985. Even when the regime was placed on a statutory footing (as a consequence of an anticipated ruling from the European Commission that the regime breached competition law) details of the new regulatory system were outlined only in secondary legislation which could not be amended by Parliament.

In 1980 a campaign was initiated by the National Union of Agricultural and Allied Workers (NUAAW) to have the herbicide 2,4,5-T banned. This began as a health and safety at work issue but rapidly expanded to a campaign for the protection of the environment and the general public. In support of the campaign the NUAAW conducted its own research into ill health, essentially an executive activity, directly challenging the advisory committee's expert assessment of the hazards posed by the chemical. The campaign was unsuccessful, except in so far as a number of local authorities banned the use of 2,4,5-T by their own employees, but it helped to raise a series of more fundamental questions about the regulatory system during the rest of the decade, concerning, for example, the UK's research policy in this area, its exclusion of wider dimensions of risk, and its habit of representing a wide range of social and political decisions as technical imperatives. Yet the only channels for expressing many of these concerns were through the media, the Parliamentary agricultural select committee and via other non-government institutions such as the British Medical Association. During the late 1980s, some of the large food retailers responded to public anxieties about agrochemical use and regulation and, to some extent, have bypassed official regulatory controls through the imposition of stricter controls on their own suppliers that is officially required (for example by demanding lower residue levels than legally necessary and by avoiding some pest control products altogether).

Finally, the neoliberal conviction that the market should determine development underpinned the government's reluctance to support new technologies in the emerging pollution control industry. Moreover the sluggish regulatory system was slow at sending signals to industry about the need to innovate. Industrial leads in innovation in Flue Gas Desulphurisation equipment, for example, were taken elsewhere, most notably in Germany, in part as a consequence of the government's prevarication on the whole issue of transboundary air pollution.

In many respects, however, European Union membership provided a countervailing force to the above tendencies. Increasing quantities of European environmental legislation introduced tensions, not only because of the possible financial implications of Community legislation, but also because the policy approaches favoured by the EU conflicted with traditional British approaches. For instance, in the case of point-source emissions to water the UK has traditionally favoured water quality standards rather than the Continental preference for fixed emission limits, in part because the UK's short and fast flowing rivers are effective at dispersing pollution. Furthermore, EU legislation has also acted as a catalyst for greater centralisation in pollution control since Directives have usually required emissions monitoring and data assembly which traditionally have been neglected in the UK. Indeed, many European Union initiatives have obliged the British government to explain and justify British control procedures that were traditionally implicit or largely rhetorical. This has allowed a broader context of accountability in domestic policy and it has opened up a debate about established practices and alternative strategies of environmental protection. (Haigh 1987)

These processes began to dovetail with the government's domestic agenda. Government demands that regulation be shown to be cost-effective could not be met within traditional uncodified approaches to policy implementation. Moreover, the realisation that site-inspection based regulation was a free form of consultancy, and a general hostility to local government (who were responsible for some aspects of pollution control), began to catalyze structural changes to the regulatory system as the 1990s approached towards more formal, centralised and legalistic forms of control.

The above trends and pressures have had a number of implications for public participation in the UK. Many of the domestic changes introduced by the Thatcher administration effectively reduced levels of formal political access, especially due to deregulation of the planning system and, to some extent, diminished consultation opportunities for environmental interests. Nevertheless a number of new opportunity structures arose. NGOs were able to take advantage of both the increased transparency and centralisation of pollution control and the conflicts between the EU and the UK government to influence both policy itself and wider political opinion. For example, during the run up to privatisation of the water utilities in the late 1980s, when the environmental consequences of the privatisation proposals were of rising political significance, Friends of the Earth were able to show that the UK breached EU regulations for drinking water quality. As a consequence of informal collaboration between FoE and DG XI, European court proceedings were initiated against the UK government. These and other rifts between the EU and the UK relating to air quality, river quality, bathing water quality, transboundary air pollution and environmental impact assessment were used strategically by environmental groups to foster the UK's label as the 'dirty man of Europe'.

Environmental groups also became increasingly adept at using the media to raise and promote environmental issues, for example through the use of powerful images and symbols that fed media interest in drama and human interest stories. Public engagement was also opened up a little by a new system of Parliamentary Select Committees which enabled environmental groups to promote their views in public fora, challenge prevailing policy orthodoxy, and appraise the evidence of official agencies, especially in policy arenas such as agriculture, energy and transport where environmental groups' influence in policy-making is minimal.

Protest was also an effective means of shifting policy trajectories. For example, in 1981 plans to explore sites for disposal of high-level waste were scrapped after militant local protests took place. Similarly sea dumping of nuclear waste was abandoned in 1983 after highly visible action by Greenpeace and the refusal to dump waste by the National Union of Seamen. As noted earlier, exploratory investigation of four potential sites for shallow disposal of low-level nuclear waste was exempted from the inquiry system in the mid-1980s. At one of the sites in Billingham the proposed repository was dropped after intense local opposition and protest in 1985 persuaded ICI, the owners of the site, to withdraw their cooperation with NIREX (the quasi-state institution responsible for nuclear waste disposal) In 1987, immediately before the general election, the government withdrew its plans for shallow waste disposal altogether after local opposition at the remaining three sites persuaded the government that continuing with policy might be an electoral liability. (Blowers 1995).

To summarise, throughout the 1980s, government-led improvements in environmental protection were rare unless forced by European legislation or by matters outside of the government's day to day control. Yet by 1988 the increasing force of European regulation, the pressure of public opinion, media interest, and intensifying NGO activities began to find resonance in government. These forces culminated in September 1988 with the apparent conversion of the Prime Minister to matters environmental when she made a speech to the Royal Society in which she underlined the credibility of global environmental threats. The speech was significant, partly because the Thatcher administration had appeared so antagonistic to environmental issues during the previous nine years but also because a commitment from the apex of the executive sent a clear message of conversion and expectation to both the UK policy-making apparatus and the wider public

3.4 Globalisation, Fragmentation and Policy Reconstitution: 1988-1990s.

During the 1990s, global and science-driven environmental risk discourses begun to assume a far more important place in political and corporate awareness. Aspects of 'ecological modernisation' (*cf* Hajer 1995) such as the precautionary principle and integrated pollution control were recognised rhetorically if not entirely in practice. At the same time, the growth of market cultures within the UK continued apace as more and more state institutions were either privatised or were run on market-orientated principles. Processes of state disengagement have also occurred as part of a separate though related trend involving a continued rolling back of the sphere of influence of government in economic activity. This process of fragmentation has occurred at the same time as public participation has been shifted from a politically articulated mode to the idea of agency through individual consumption in the marketplace;

changes underpinned by wider ideological shifts involving the political reconstruction of citizenship in the UK. (Gamble 1988)

Thatcher's characterisation of the key environmental issues as globalised and scientifically defined at the 1988 Royal Society meeting was opportunistic for a number of reasons. Firstly, a range of domestic environmental issues were prominent immediately prior to Thatcher's speech and defining the critical problems as global finessed demands for substantive local action in so far as the UK could take the lead on organising and conducting research into, for example global warming, without immediate adverse financial or political consequences. Secondly, there was competition from other industrialised nations for gaining an influential position in the international negotiations that would be necessary to tackle global environmental issues and the Thatcher speech can be interpreted as a means of favourably positioning the UK in this context. Thirdly, the bid for leadership in negotiating responses to global environmental change was also a useful opportunity to challenge EU sovereignty and influence over the UK which, at that time, had emerged as a topic of considerable political friction. Finally, the speech was made to a scientific institution - the Royal Society - and was in part a means of responding to pressures from the scientific community over the deteriorating relative position and funding of UK scientific research.

The renewed political and public interest following Thatcher's speech was reflected in an extremely rapid rise in membership for environmental groups, and heightened media interest. In 1990 a major statement of UK environmental policy strategy *This Common Inheritance* was published but despite considerable expectation the paper outlined few new commitments. Nevertheless a belated recognition of the structural nature of environmental problems, aspirations towards cross-agency integration of regulatory functions, and the greening of government ministries was evident. Furthermore, since the late 1980s the Department of the

Environment began to reposition itself from an agent of State influence and control over external environmental commitments to an agent of environmental commitments within government. This has led to a greater degree of conflict, or at least publicly visible conflict, between different government departments and agents, for example between the DoE, on the one hand, and the Treasury, Department of Trade and Industry and Department of Transport on the other. (Wynne *et al* 1996) There is also an awareness that existing regulatory policies have generally failed to push or send signals to industry about the desirability of technological innovation. New regulatory programmes such as the Integrated Pollution Control regime have been designed, in part, to move away from end-of-pipe solutions and encourage the adoption of cleaner technologies, although it is too early to assess the efficacy of these types of policy innovations.

Greater representation of moderate environmental interests in some policy sectors is also evident. Informal contact between NGOs and officials in the Department of the Environment increased during the 1990s as well as more formal types of involvement. For example, Tom Burke, the Director of the Green Alliance and previously Friends of the Earth's Executive Director, was appointed as 'specialist advisor' to the Secretary of State at the Department of the Environment. In other sensitive areas of policy there have also been some relatively novel forms of public engagement. For example, in agricultural biotechnology, an area where the industry has been particularly anxious that the development of the technology commands public legitimacy, one of the UK biotechnology regulatory committees, the Advisory Committee on Releases in the Environment (ACRE) (established in 1990) contains a representative from an environmental lobbying group. Nevertheless, risk issues in agricultural biotechnology remain narrowly defined with ACRE only concerned with immediate technical dimensions of risk. There is, for example, no clear route of expression for broader concerns about ethical issues, the general trajectory of agricultural strategies or questions of need. In 1994 an initiative to engage with public criticism was taken through a National Consensus Conference on Plant Biotechnology although the conference had no powers to alter policy, nor was there any requirement on the part of the industry or the legislative and regulatory systems to engage with the conference recommendations. Indeed Lord Howie, chair of the Lords Select Committee on Biotechnology stated at the conference that Parliament would not be influenced by the report in any significant way. (Purdue 1996)

Programmes of privatisation, deregulation (and reregulation) and deference to the market continued to induce cultural changes to traditional forms of British regulation. For example, in the process of transforming the energy, water and telecommunications utilities into private companies a range of unanticipated issues arose. Public trust in the new companies fell far below that which had existed when they were in the public sector, and consequently pressures for more formal and rigorous regulation and greater accountability increased. The 1990 Environmental Protection Act, for example, established a framework of integrated pollution control that involved provisions for providing public information on polluting activities. Also in 1992 the government announced its intention to establish an Environment Agency (eventually introduced in 1996) which would combine the regulatory functions of the National Rivers Authority, the Pollution Inspectorate (responsible for emissions to air) and the waste regulatory functions of local authorities. These shifts are, however, only beginning and do not compare to the codified, formal approaches to regulation found in other countries. In areas such as carbon dioxide stabilization and CFC replacement, traditional forms of gaining industry compliance have been resorted to.

Privatisation also dispensed with the central planning role of quasi-government bodies such as the Central Electricity Generating Board and effectively turned responsibility for most aspects of policy over to the private sector. One consequence has been that the focus on the inquiry system as a vehicle for public engagement in UK energy policy has diminished markedly. The UK government established a regulator for the energy sector, but this was concerned primarily with protecting the commercial viability of the electricity industry and encouraging competition. Most aspects of energy policy were either uncatered for (for example security of supply considerations) or the responsibility of the private sector which was far more fragmented. Aspects of energy policy that had strong environmental components, for example energy conservation considerations, were, as far as the government were concerned, something to be catered for by market forces. One fortuitous fallout of privatisation has been the freeze and perhaps the demise of development in civil nuclear power. The attempt to sell-off nuclear power to the private sector was stopped dead by the financial world's insistence on full disclosure of accounts and the subsequent exposure of far greater costs and liabilities than had been officially admitted.

Government has also shifted to a focus on individual consumption in the marketplace rather than policy regulation as a means of dealing with environmental problems. Since 1991 the UK government has pressed the theme of individual responsibility to encourage the public to reduce carbon dioxide emissions through domestic energy efficiency measures rather than through regulation. Similarly, following the 1992 Earth summit, for example, the Department of the Environment has identified a strong role for individual action in achieving environmental change, promoting a scheme named 'Going for Green' which has emphasized the provision of information to the public so that as individuals they can take action to achieve environmental change. In the UK's 1994 sustainable development strategy document the government claimed that one of the most powerful ways in which individuals can influence environmental matters is through the products they buy. (Simmonds 1995)

The general growth of market cultures in the UK was also reflected in the privatisation of large state-funded research laboratories and a shift away from government funding of 'near market' research. Where government continued to fund research, a greater role for industry in dictating research priorities is becoming evident, (Edgerton & Hughes 1989) reflected, for example in the 1995 transfer of the Office of Science and Technology from the Cabinet Office to the Department of Trade and Industry. (Lea 1995) Furthermore, whole subsections of government departments have been set up as 'Next Steps Agencies' responsible for their own budgets, expected to be managed in a similar way to private sector institutions, and sometimes expected to raise their own revenue.

As far as technology policy is concerned government activity has continued to be extremely limited although there have been a few initiatives. For example, the Department of Trade and Industry began a three year programme in 1990 worth £5 million to encourage environmental innovation in areas such as clean incineration and plastics recovery. Similar though smaller research initiatives have also been taken by the Science and Engineering Research Council and the Department of the Environment. (Wynne *et al* 1996) An attempt by Parliament to establish Parliamentary Office of Science and Technology along the same sort of lines as the US Office of Technology Assessment and other similar initiatives in Europe was refused public funding by the government. However, an organisation was instead established in 1989 by the Parliamentary and Scientific Committee with private support. The Parliamentary Office of Science and Technology (POST) operates as a charity and is funded by large technology-based companies, institutions such as the Royal Society and charitable trusts. (Norton 1996)

These trends described above have had several implications for the strategies taken by environmental groups to influence environmental policy processes. The prominent global, science-driven issues have not been pushed exclusively by the NGOs. Concern about ozone depletion, for example, (which had first emerged as an issue in the early 1970s) was elevated predominantly by the scientific community after researchers at the British Antarctic Survey reported findings of a dramatic decrease in ozone concentrations over the South Pole. Similarly anthropogenic climate change as an environmental issue was driven by the scientific community. Environmental groups did not become involved in climate change and ozone depletion issues until the late 1980s and found themselves in the position of reinforcing and responding to rather than elevating those issues onto the political agenda. The role of national environmental groups is also somewhat more ambivalent now that 'the environment' is more firmly established on the political and social agenda.

At least some environmental groups have shifted away from only attempting to influence State regulatory processes and have directed some of their energies to lobbying industry directly as well and by attempting to influence financial and consumer markets. For example, Greenpeace has been active in attempting to change industry's response to global warming by mobilizing the power of the financial sector as an agent of change by framing global warming in terms of liabilities. (Wynne *et al* 1996) Friends of the Earth was also quite active in calling for a consumer boycott of CFC aerosols in 1987. Environmental groups have also began to undertake activities that are, or were essentially executive functions. Greenpeace, for example, were invited to prosecute a company found to be illegally venting CFCs and brought the health implications of continued ozone depletion to the attention of the medical profession and the general public. (Wynne *et al* 1996)

Interestingly the environmental NGOs have begun attempting to directly influence private innovation processes with a focus on promoting technical solutions to environmental problems. For example, after the UK government officially recognized that CFCs were responsible for ozone depletion they refused to introduce regulations to ensure proper control of such substances. Greenpeace UK teamed up with a German manufacturer to produce an innovative hydrocarbon-based refrigerator. These measures have contributed to a more general shift in the antagonistic relationships between industry and environmental groups, and industry have increasingly approached NGOs for advice on generating 'solutions' to environmental problems. (Elkington 1996)

It is not entirely clear what implications the trends that can be identified in the 1990s (in terms of the fragmentation of the State, a greater focus on globalised environmental issues, a discursive shift to an individualised, consumer-led form of agency, and changing NGO strategies and opportunities) imply for public engagement more generally. There may well be tensions associated with diminishing agency on the part of the public as formal channels for public engagement in the political process recede and the relevant environmental issues are defined by government, industry and at least some NGOs as ever more technically complex and science-driven. For example, in the early 1990s, there was an upsurge in grass-roots protest over the development of roads and these new actors have shunned both formal channels of influence and representation and the national environmental groups. At Twyford Down in Hampshire, for example - a site including ancient monuments and rare habitat protected by special status designations - a proposed bypass was challenged both through the public inquiry system by the local community and national environmental groups and by the EU (as a consequence of a judgment by DG X1 that the UK had failed to conduct an Environmental Impact Assessment) whilst grass-roots organisations (and later local residents) occupied the site, repeatedly clashing with police and security guards. The movement emerging around the anti-roads protests (over 200 local groups were established within a year of the Twyford Down protest) was concerned not just with local environmental consequences of roads but with far more general and moral arguments about economic development and the type of society that the road building programme reflected. It is, however unclear in what way these more recent developments might be linked to any of the wider trends of the 1990s, especially since the history of British environmentalism has seen sustained grass-roots protest on a number of different issues.

Despite the more recent trends towards greater integration of environmental priorities into other government policies and shifts towards cross-agency integration, British environmental science and technology policy is still fragmented, conducted largely at a sectoral level and increasingly the responsibility of, or orientated towards, the private sector. Influence in the various policy sectors remains dominated by industry and elite groups of experts. Even though there has been a small opening up of formal avenues of influence for moderate environmental groups in some aspects of policy, these have rarely been sufficient to allow civic interests scope for shifting or reframing policy trajectories. In sectors such as research and development, policy remains entirely closed to almost any form of formal public participation. It will be worthwhile exploring the dynamics and tensions associated with demands for public participation in different policy sectors and to consider the implications for future innovation and policy reconstitution.

References

Blowers, A. (1987) 'Transition or Transformation? - Environmental Policy Under Thatcher', *Public Administration*, Vol. 65, pp. 277-294

Blowers, A. (1995) 'Nuclear Waste Disposal: A Technical Problem in Search of a Political Solution', in T. Gray (ed) *UK Environmental Policy in the 1990s*, Macmillan Press, London.

Edgerton, D. & Hughes, K. (1989) 'The Poverty of Science: A Critical Analysis of Scientific and Industrial Policy Under Mrs Thatcher', *Public Administration*, Vol. 67, pp. 419-433

Elkington, J. (1996) 'Green World Alliance PLC', *The Guardian*, 20 November 1996

Elzinga, A. & Jamison, A. (1995) 'Changing Policy Agendas in Science and Technology', in S. Jasanoff *et al* (eds) *Handbook of Science and Technology Studies*, Sage, London.

Everest, D. A. (1990) 'The Provision of Expert Advice to Government on Environmental Matters: the Role of Advisory Committees', *Science and Public Affairs*, Vol. 4, pp. 17-40

Gamble, A. (1988) *The Free Economy and the Strong State: The Politics of Thatcherism*, Macmillan, London.

Grove-White, R. (1991) *The UK's Environmental Movement and UK Political Culture*, Report to EURES, November 1991, Centre for the Study of Environmental Change, Lancaster University.

Haigh, N. (1987) *EEC Environmental Policy and Britain*, 2nd edition, Longman, London.

Hajer, M. (1995) *The Politics of Environmental Discourse: Ecological Modernisation and the Policy Process*, Clarendon Press, Oxford.

Hutton, W. (1995) *The State We're In*, Cape, London.

Jordan, G. & Richardson, J. (1982) 'The British Policy Style or the Logic of Negotiation', in J. Richardson (ed) *Policy Styles in Western Europe*, Allen & Unwin, London.

Laffin, M. (1986) Professionalism and Policy: The Role of the Professions in the Central-Local Government Relationship, Gower, Aldershot.

Lea, W. (1995) *Transfer of the OST to the DTI and UK Science Policy*, House of Commons Research Paper 95/103, London.

Levin, P. H. (1979) 'Highway Inquiries: A Study in Governmental Responsiveness', *Public Administration*, Vol. 57, pp. 21-50

Lowe, P. & Flynn, A. (1989) 'Environmental Politics and Policy in the 1980s', in J. Mohan (ed) *The Political Geography of Contemporary Britain*, Macmillan, London.

Lowe, P & Goyer, J. (1983) *Environmental Groups in Politics*, Allen & Unwin, London.

Newby, H. (1990) 'Ecology, Amenity and Society', *Town Planning Review*, Vol. 61, No. 1, pp. 3-10

Norton, M. (1996) 'Parliamentary Technology Assessment in the UK', *International Journal of Technology Management*, Vol. 11, Nos 5/6, pp. 581-588

O'Riordan, T. & Weale, A. (1989) 'Administrative Reorganisation and Policy Change: The Case of Her Majesty's Inspectorate of Pollution', *Public Administration*, Vol. 67, pp. 277-294

Purdue, D. (1996) 'Contested Expertise: Plant Biotechnology and Social Movements', *Science as Culture*, Vol. 5, Part 4, pp. 526-545

Rhodes, R. A. W. (1988) *Beyond Westminster and Whitehall*, Unwin Hyman, London.

Rudig, W. (1995) 'Between Moderation and Marginalization: Environmental Radicalism in Britain', in B. R. Taylor (ed) *Ecological Resistance Movements: The Global Emergence of Radical and Popular Environmentalism*, SUNY, Albany.

Saward. M. (1992) 'The Civil Nuclear Network in Britain', in D. Marsh & R. A. W. Rhodes (eds) *Policy Networks in British government*, Clarendon Press, Oxford.

Simmonds, P. (1995) 'Green Consumerism: Blurring the Boundary Between Public and Private', in S. Edgell et al (eds) *Debating the Future of the Public Sphere: Transforming the Public and Private Domains in Free Market Societies*, Avebury, Aldershot.

Smith, J. M. (1989) 'Changing Agendas and Policy Communities: Agricultural Issues in the 1930s and the 1980s', *Public Administration*, Vol. 67, pp. 149-165

Tuxworth, B. (1996) 'From Environment to Sustainability: Surveys and Analysis of Local Agenda 21 Process Development in UK Local Authorities', *Local Environment*, Vol. 1, No. 3, pp. 277-297

Vig, N. (1968) *Science and Technology in British Politics*, Pergamon, London.

Whitelegg, (1989) 'Transport Policy: Off the Rails?' in J. Mohan (ed) *The Political Geography of Contemporary Britain*, Macmillan, London.

Wynne, B. (1982) *Rationality and Ritual: The Windscale Inquiry and Nuclear Decisions in Britain*, BSHS, Chlafont St Giles.

Wynne, B. *et al* (1996, forthcoming) 'Institutional Cultures and the Management of Global Environmental Risks in the UK', in W. Clark *et al* (eds) *Learning to Manage Global Environmental Risks*.

Wynne, B. & Crouch, D. (1991) *Responsiveness of Science and Technology Institutions to Environmental Change - A UK Case Study*, Report to OECD, December 1991, Centre for the Study of Environmental Change and Centre for Science Studies and Science Policy, Lancaster University.

Contributors

Andrew Jamison, Research Unit in Technology and Society, Department of Development and Planning, Aalborg University, Denmark

Erik Baark, Institute of Technology and Social Sciences, Technical University of Denmark

Per Østby, Center for Technology and Society, University of Trondheim, Norway

Leonardas Rinkevicius, Department of Public Administration, Kaunas University of Technology, Lithuania

Ørn Jonsson, Fisheries Research Institute, University of Iceland

Jose Andringa and Johan Schot, Center for Studies of Science, Technology and Society, University of Twente, the Netherlands

Patrick van Zwanenberg, Center for the Study of Environmental Change, University of Lancaster, United Kingdom